PORTRAIT OF A CHEF

PORTRAIT OF A CHEF

THE LIFE OF

ALEXIS SOYER

Sometime Chef to the Reform Club

BY

HELEN MORRIS

Oxford Toronto Melbourne Cape Town

OXFORD UNIVERSITY PRESS

1980

Oxford University Press, Walton Street, Oxford OX2 6DP

OXFORD LONDON GLASGOW
NEW YORK TORONTO MELBOURNE WELLINGTON
KUALA LUMPUR SINGAPORE JAKARTA HONG KONG TOKYO
DELHI BOMBAY CALCUTTA MADRAS KARACHI
NAIROBI DAR ES SALAAM CAPE TOWN

Copyright Helen Morris 1938
First published by Cambridge University Press 1938
First issued as an Oxford University Press paperback 1980

British Cataloguing in Publication Data
Morris, Helen, b. 1909
Portrait of a chef.
1. Soyer, Alexis
2. Cooks – Biography
I. Title
642'.47'0924   TX649.S|
ISBN 0-19-285094-6

Reproduced, printed and bound in Great Britain by
Cox & Wyman Ltd, Reading

For

M. C. S. *and* C. G. S.

ACKNOWLEDGMENTS

IT is a pleasure to offer my thanks to all who have helped me in the preparation of this Biography. For information on particular points I am indebted to Commander J. N. Benbow, R.N. (Retd.), Secretary of the Royal Humane Society; to Mr S. J. Benham, whose grandfather equipped the Reform Club's kitchens in 1841; to Mr F. S. Blackwell of Messrs Crosse and Blackwell; to Mr T. Burgess, Superintendent of Kensal Green Cemetery; to Mr C. E. Carrington; to Mr E. M. Crosse; to Mr Christopher Hobhouse; to Mr John Saltmarsh and to Major C. H. Massé, R.A.S.C.

The staff of the Cambridge University Library have given me every possible assistance, and I must thank in particular Mr G. de Fraine and Mr H. L. Pink for their patience with my endless enquiries.

Finally I would like to assure Mr Christopher Morris that without his untiring advice and encouragement I should never have completed this *Portrait of a Chef*.

H. M.

August 1938

CONTENTS

Alexis Soyer, engraving after a portrait by his wife

PROLOGUE

'In number of dishes and change of meat the nobility of England (whose cooks are for the most part musical-headed Frenchmen and strangers) do most exceed.'

HARRISON, *Description of England*, 1577

AMONG the less eminent Victorians was a man who wrote a book which sold a quarter of a million copies and who was caricatured in one of Thackeray's novels; who figured more often in the pages of *Punch* than many a Cabinet Minister; who was a dandy and a 'card'; who saved the lives of thousands of soldiers and benefited hundreds of thousands; who drew the breath of his being from the French Romantics and who won the respect of Victorian England for his practical resourcefulness and powers of administration. He was only a cook, but he cooked for princes and for paupers, and his cooking had not a little to do with the growth of a great political party.

A Frenchman by birth, he lived most of his life in England; he wrote poems and cookery books and a ballet and innumerable letters to *The Times*. He invented—among hundreds of other things—sauces, drinks, patent pots and pans and kettles and tea-pots, an appliance for rescuing the drowning, entrée dishes, pantomime illusions, naval kitchens, a device for keeping money in the heels of dress boots and a stove which has been used in the British army for over eighty years.

He created a dish costing a hundred guineas—and a soup-kitchen which produced good soup at three-farthings a quart. He organised great banquets for visiting celebrities—and a dinner one Christmas Day for twenty thousand of the poorest of London's poor. He cooked recherché dinners worthy of Lucullus—and exhausted his health in the Crimea turning army rations of salt pork into palatable food. He sent a

1

special messenger to fetch ortolans from Paris for one particular dish—and at the Government's request drew up scales of diet for emigrants and military hospitals. He was the boon companion of the greatest gourmets of the town—and the respected fellow-worker of Florence Nightingale. He cooked a banquet for the Prince Consort and all the mayors of England—and fed the starving Irish in the hungry 'forties. He produced with equal promptness grandiose fantastic schemes and practical plans worked out to the last detail. He designed a magic stove which could be carried in the pocket—and planned the immense kitchens of the Reform Club.

He was vain, a poseur, a fop, an eccentric—he was gay, witty, a good singer, a much-admired raconteur—a brilliant inventor and a magnificent organiser—he was the kindest of friends, and the most generous and loyal of masters and servants.

His name was Alexis Soyer.

CHAPTER I

EARLY LIFE

'*If* you 'ave got the Touch—mark you, I only say if—but *if* you 'ave anything like the Genuine Touch, you're provided for for life. *An'* further...you 'old your neighbours, friends and employers in the 'ollow of your 'and....Everything which a man *is* depends on what 'e puts inside 'im,...A good cook's a King of men—besides being thunderin' well off if 'e don't drink. It's the only sure business in the whole round world.'

KIPLING, *His Gift*

SOME twenty-five miles north-east of Paris is a small town, Meaux-en-Brie, which every gastronome should honour. Here is made the delicious Fromage de Brie, and here, on 14th October 1809, was born Alexis Benoît Soyer, the third and youngest son of a small shopkeeper.

His mother, ambitious for her baby, was determined to make him a priest. Even as a tiny child, Alexis showed a love of music, and soon developed a good ear and a true voice; his uncle was Grand Vicar of the cathedral school founded at Meaux by Bossuet at the end of the seventeenth century, and when Alexis was nine years old he was sent there as a chorister. He found the singing pure joy, but he had soon had enough of confinement and discipline, and decided that he would not for the world become an ecclesiastic. His mother refused to take him away from the school, despite his constant complaints, so Alexis made up his mind to get himself expelled. Various slight misdemeanours were overlooked, but one night he went too far. He persuaded some friends to help him ring the great bell of the church at midnight—the local fire alarm. The whole town was aroused; the garrison turned out—and Alexis was expelled from school. Perhaps it was this early success that made him all his life so deplorably devoted to the practical joke.

3

He was now twelve and, apart from his determination to be done with the Church as a vocation, did not feel inclined to any particular career. His elder brother Philippe was a cook in Paris, and his brother Louis a cabinet-maker; neither occupation appealed to Alexis. But being in disgrace at home, he went to stay with Philippe while he hunted for work, and after trying various jobs for a week or two at a time he became apprenticed, almost by accident, to his brother's trade.

For four years Alexis worked *chez Grignon*, in the Rue Vivienne, and he could have had no better school. It was not perhaps as famous as Véry's, nor as ostentatious as the *Rocher de Cancale*, with its thirty-four soups and its hundred and twelve dishes of fish, but Grignon's twenty dining-rooms were so many temples of gastronomy, served with due solemnity by clients, cooks and waiters. A high authority declared that the 'entremets and hors d'œuvres were unexceptionable'. The head waiter apologised once to a diner because a dish would take some time to dress; 'Mais', he added, 'Monsieur ne s'ennuiera point.' He produced the *carte*, a neatly bound octavo volume. 'Voilà une lecture très agréable.'

It was considered infinitely more important to satisfy a real gourmet than to make a profit. One client, thinking his dinner worthy of the best wine on the list, chose the most expensive, a *Clos de Vougeot* at twelve francs. The waiter took the order, then hesitated and came back to the table. The *Clos de Vougeot*, he said, was excellent, but if Monsieur wished the best wine, the very best wine, he should choose the *Richebourg* at a mere five francs. This was the spirit in which Alexis received his early training, and which always inspired him.

He got on so well that when only sixteen he was engaged as second cook by a well-known restaurateur and caterer, Douix, of the Boulevard des Italiens, and there he often got into absurd scrapes. Douix supplied not only supper but also table ornaments of china and glass for parties and balls. On one occasion Alexis was responsible for dessert, and also for the safe return of these ornaments. After supper had been served, he and the other young cooks sang and supped and drank, and it was not until one o'clock that they set out for home, carefully balancing their wooden trays heaped with china, glass and silver.

It was a cold frosty night, and the fresh air made Alexis jollier than ever. He strode ahead, singing lustily,

> Ah! voilà la vie, la vie, la vie, suivie,
> Ah! voilà la vie, que les moines font,
> V'la, v'la—v'la—

but his head began to swim, he sat down, yawned, thought himself at home, lay down and went to sleep. Waking with a start, he sprang up, forgetting the tray, and ran back to the café, where the others were waiting and wondering what had become of him. There was a shout of laughter when he appeared—he had forgotten not only his tray but his trousers! Luckily the name Douix was on the tray, and the police eventually returned both china and inexpressibles, but not until Alexis had been well rated by his master, and not until he was heartily tired of being asked by his mates to which regiment he belonged, and if he always preferred to bivouac in the open field.

High spirits and love of jesting did not imply irresponsibility, for in 1826 he was made *Premier de l'Administration* at Douix's, with twelve cooks under him. Most of them were considerably older than Alexis, and as they naturally resented being ordered about by a boy of seventeen, at first they made things a little difficult. But not for long; Alexis already had the good-humoured air and the pleasant manner which throughout his life was to make his fellow-workers devoted to him.

All his spare time was spent at the *Théâtre des Variétés*; an excellent mimic, he could send his friends into fits of laughter by imitations of the celebrated comedians of the day—Brunet, Odry, Levasseur. Throughout his life Soyer desired above everything the applause and approval of his fellows; he loved bright colours and rich stuffs; he had a talent for mimicry, a fine voice, and a good ear; he seemed—to himself at any rate —ideally fitted for the stage. Philippe thought that it would be madness to abandon the profession in which Alexis had made such a brilliant start, and spent long hours of argument persuading him to stick to the kitchen. Alexis took his brother's advice, but the theatre was always his favourite recreation, and during the years to come the characteristics which might have served him well as an actor expressed themselves in other ways. Deprived of opportunity of wearing fine clothes on the stage, he took to dressing in eccentric costumes of his own design in ordinary life; he continually organised concerts and 'sing-songs', often at most unlikely times and in most unsuitable places; his desire for admiration and attention expressed itself in a thousand ways, of which one of the most amusing was a constant stream of letters to *The Times*.

At the end of July 1830 the Foreign Minister, Prince Polignac, had arranged to give a grand entertainment at the Foreign Office, for which extra cooks were engaged, Soyer among them. Unfortunately, Polignac had also arranged to publish at the same time the hated *ordonnances* of St Cloud which caused the July revolution and the end of the reign of Charles X. The enraged mob forced the gates of the courtyard, and burst into the kitchens. Two of Soyer's confrères were struck down before his eyes, and the other cooks fled. With great presence of mind Soyer leapt upon a table, and began to sing *La Marseillaise* in his fine clear voice. The song was taken up by the rioters, and he was seized and carried shoulder-high in the van of the crowd, becoming their leader instead of their victim, while, as he said, 'toutes ces somptueuses préparations furent doublement consommées par eux'.

6

This exciting experience was unsettling; Alexis found himself out of a job and began to think of accepting Philippe's pressing invitations to join him at the Duke of Cambridge's in London.

These were great days for a *chef* in England; French cooking had come in with Empire furniture, and a French cook commanded high wages. The Earl of Sefton—famous for his extravagance, his gambling, his greed and his grumbling at taxation—paid Ude three hundred guineas a year for twenty years, and left him a hundred a year for life. As Grimod de la Reynière had observed, cooks no longer like Vatel[1] died for their masters, but preferred to live on them. Certainly they picked and chose their employers, and left if they were not appreciated. A salary of a thousand a year could not tempt Carême to stay with the Prince Regent—'C'est que la cuisine de son altesse royale est trop bourgeoise'—and Felix had to leave the Duke of Wellington—'I serve him a dinner which would make Ude or Francatelli burst with envy, and he says —nothing; I go out and leave him a dinner badly dressed by the cookmaid, and he says—nothing; I cannot live with such a man were he a hundred times a hero.'[2]

Every cook arranged his own (sometimes fantastic) terms of employment—one would not accompany his master to Ireland, though offered four hundred pounds a year, because there was no Italian opera in Dublin; another *chef* left because he did not agree with his master about the Reform Bill. In the Royal Household, on special occasions, the name of the *chef* who had dressed each dish was printed on the menu beside his creation. Everything was done on the grand scale. Though the Duke of Buckingham was ruined financially, he was horrified when it was suggested that as he had a French

[1] Vatel committed suicide because he thought he was not to have enough fish to serve the king properly.

[2] Wellington was no gourmet; he used to dine at the Senior United Club on a cut from the joint, and once created a great disturbance when he was charged one and threepence instead of a shilling.

chef and an English roasting-cook he might dismiss his Italian confectioner. 'Good God!' he cried, 'mayn't a man have a biscuit with his glass of sherry?'

England seemed the very place for an ambitious young cook, and early in 1831 Alexis joined his brother in London, and cooked his first dinner in England for young Prince George of Cambridge. Alexis was twenty-one, and for the rest of his life England was to be his home.

Young Soyer found London much to his taste. He worked for short periods at the Duke of Sutherland's and the Marquis of Waterford's, and then became *chef* to a Mr Lloyd of Aston Hall, near Oswestry, where he spent four happy years.

Mr Lloyd's dinners became famous, and his friends used to beg for the loan of his cook when some special entertainment was toward. Most famous cooks have jealously guarded the secrets of their cuisine, but Soyer—partly from goodness of heart and partly from delight in exhibiting his own cleverness —was always willing to explain the preparation or composition of a dish, and was for ever inventing labour-saving devices for his friends' kitchens as well as his own. Myddleton Biddulph of Chirk Castle, later Master of the Household to Queen Victoria, was one of the more epicurean of the local gentry, and his steward Charles Pierce became one of Soyer's lifelong friends.

Soyer's quick wit and his readiness to burst into song made him popular in the local inns, and when the news spread that he was in the parlour of the 'Queen's Head'—where he often met Pierce—his acquaintances crowded in till there was hardly sitting room. This was gratifying; indoors he could hold his own, but outside it was not such plain sailing. He found English sporting habits absolutely bewildering, and the local farmers regarded this queer foreigner with a good deal of suspicion.

On the first of March every year, Sir Watkin Williams Wynn was accustomed to amuse the neighbouring sportsmen by unbagging a fox, and Soyer was asked, one year, to attend. Sir Watkin, himself a great gourmand who had feasted fifteen thousand people in his park when he came of age, ought to have felt kindly towards the *chef*, but he allowed his huntsman John to unbag a dog. Away went Alexis after the 'fox', while the rest of the field roared with laughter, and the rash Soyer was soon thrown violently into a hedge.

After four years in Wales it was time to return to the centre of things. For a year Soyer was *chef* to the eccentric and gourmet Marquis of Ailsa, the former Earl of Cassilis, whose second son by marrying an illegitimate daughter of William IV had gained a marquisate for his father. In 1836 Soyer, with great reluctance, left him for a new post which was too tempting to be refused. Here he was to have the opportunity he had always longed for—a chance to plan his own kitchens on a magnificent scale, and to use his ingenuity and powers of organisation to the full. He left the marquis and became *chef de cuisine* to the Reform Club, where he was to spend a quarter of his life.

The Rt Hon. Edward Ellice, M.P. (known as 'Bear' Ellice because his money came from the Canadian fur trade) had been Whig Whip at the time of the Reform Bill. He was now anxious that the Liberal members of the reformed Parliament should have a club, and proposed that Brooks's should rebuild their club-house and admit six hundred new members. But the committee of Brooks's had had enough of Reformers— O'Connell had celebrated his election to the club by calling one of its most admired members, Lord Alvanley, 'a bloated buffoon', and when the committee had refused to expel O'Connell, sixty Whig peers had resigned *en bloc*.

After much intriguing, Liberals and Radicals led by Ellice and Sir William Molesworth founded a club of their own at 104 Pall Mall, 'to promote the social Intercourse of the Reformers of the United Kingdom', and almost at once there were a thousand members. The original club-house proved far too small, so the committee bought the houses on either side of it, with extra ground at the back, and invited several eminent architects to send in plans for a new club-house. The committee's instructions were that the Reform Club should 'surpass all others in size and magnificence' (especially the Travellers' on one side and the Carlton on the other), and the design chosen was that submitted by Charles Barry, inspired by the Farnese Palace at Rome.

While the new club was being built, the members found a temporary home at Gwydyr House, and here in 1838 Soyer had his first notable triumph. The Reformers' celebrations in honour of the queen's coronation were, as the *Morning Chronicle* remarked, 'upon the most liberal and extensive scale'. 'No expense was spared... and certainly the style in which the entertainment was conducted reflects the very highest credit upon the liberality of those to whom the management was committed.' The members brought eight hundred guests, who saw the procession from specially erected and decorated balconies. 'Scarfs, handkerchiefs and hats were waved as Her Majesty passed,' recorded the *Globe*, 'every balcony was a parterre, every window was a bouquet of loveliness and beauty.'

After the procession had passed on to the Abbey, the ladies descended from the closely packed tiers of benches to the garden, where their wide skirts of batiste or organdie, checked barège or embroidered muslin, could be shaken out, and the scarves which had been waved so enthusiastically draped again over their owners' elegant sloping shoulders. To the overtures and waltzes played by Herr Strauss and his band they strolled on the grass, the Reformers in their blue and green and maroon tail coats and their gay flowered waistcoats almost as decorative as their guests. This was precisely the sort of occasion that Soyer loved, and with what delight he must have planned and prepared the 'very splendid déjeuner à la Fourchette'[1] which sustained the company during their long wait for the return of the newly crowned queen.

[1] *Morning Chronicle*, 29th June 1838.

The Reformers were always ready to experiment, and though their display of 'the word "Victoria" in variegated lamps' upon the princess's eighteenth birthday had been considered in doubtful taste, they again employed what the *Morning Chronicle* described as 'all-powerful and all-brilliant gas'. It was reported that the 'club building, the occupiers of which had excelled almost every other club in the display of ladies in the balconies during the morning, was not less distinguished by its illuminations at night'. These consisted of 'a crown, V.R. and wreath, and Victoria, all on a colossal scale, in jets of gas'.[1]

Barry designed the kitchen premises of the new building in close consultation with the *chef*; 'the enthusiasm and knowledge of M. Soyer', wrote the architect's son, 'were allowed full scope', and Soyer's suggestions and many of his own inventions were incorporated in the plans. On 1st March 1841, Soyer took possession of the finest kitchens in London. The members might stalk proudly through the marble halls above, but, in the words of a contemporary, 'it is in the lower regions, where Soyer reigns supreme, that the true glories of the Reform Club consist.... Heliogabulus himself', he goes on, 'never gloated over such a kitchen, for steam is here introduced and made to supply the part of man. In state the great dignitary sits, and issues his inspiring orders to a body of lieutenants, each of whom has pretensions to be considered a *chef* in himself.... Soyer is indeed the glory of the edifice, the *genius loci*.'

Indeed, it was often suggested that the *chef* was a greater force for political unity than any party leader, and that the popularity of the club was due as much to the excellence of the cuisine as to the purity of the Liberalism professed. Even before he had his new kitchen to aid him in performing miracles, Soyer's reputation had begun to grow. The words 'reformed cooking' conjure up nowadays a depressing vision of nut cutlets and calory-counting fanatics; a hundred years

[1] *Globe*, 29th June 1838.

ago their implications were very different. Soyer's prodigious powers of invention enabled him to present a continual succession of new delicacies to the enraptured members, and the praise with which each was greeted seemed to stimulate him to further flights of fancy.

Ordinary members were not neglected; an admirable club dinner was supplied for a shilling or so, instead of the more expensive meal usual in earlier clubs. At this time, too, a custom originated which was observed at the centenary banquet of the club in 1936, that after an especially good dinner the *chef* should appear in the dining-room, while the members drink his health and he drinks theirs.

CHAPTER II

EMMA JONES

'A good wife is Heaven's last best gift to man—his angel and minister of graces innumerable—his gem of many virtues—his casket of jewels; her voice is sweet music—her smiles, his brightest day—her kiss, the guardian of his innocence—her arms, the pale of his safety, the balm of his health, the balsam of his life—her industry, his surest wealth—her economy, his safest steward—her lips, his faithful counsellors—her bosom, the softest pillow of his cares.'

JEREMY TAYLOR

As *chef* to the Reform Club, Soyer was very comfortably off and could well afford to marry. Not having a high opinion of English women as wives, he thought of sending his portrait, with the offer of his hand, to an old love in Paris; he was advised to commission a M. Simonau to paint him. This Simonau, a Flemish pupil of Baron Gros, had settled in England twenty years before, and founded an academy of drawing and painting. Going to his studio to arrange for sittings, Alexis met there Simonau's pupil and stepdaughter, Emma Jones, and straightway fell head over heels in love. He gave up all idea of sending the portrait to Paris; it was useful only as an excuse for constant and lengthy visits to the studio to see Emma.

Emma Jones was only twenty-six, but was already well known for her popular crayon portraits. Her mother had brought her, as an infant prodigy, to Simonau's studio, when Emma was so young that only the urgent entreaties of Mrs Jones induced him to accept the little girl as a pupil. After she had been with him six months, he was so impressed by her talent that he gave up his other pupils and devoted himself to her alone. 'Before the age of twelve,' it is recorded, 'she had drawn more than a hundred portraits from life with surprising fidelity.' At the same time she had lessons in music from Ancot, a friend of Rossini and Weber, and Weber heard her play a passage from *Der Freischutz* so brilliantly that he prophesied a splendid career for her as a professional musician.

Simonau married Mrs Jones, Emma's mother, in 1820, making Emma his daughter as well as his pupil, and there were continual discussions as to whether she should become an artist or a musician. While they were holidaying at Dunkirk, Emma herself settled the question. Looking out of the window, she saw some children blowing bubbles, and immediately drew a sketch of them on the wall with charcoal. It was so clever and spirited that even her mother, who had been eager to have her daughter a musician, was forced to agree that such a talent should not be neglected. A picture from this sketch was later sold for sixty pounds.

Unlike most remarkably clever infants, Emma became an equally remarkable woman, handsome, accomplished, witty, gay, musical—altogether the very person to fascinate Soyer. He fell in love as he did everything—impetuously and with all his heart; he showed his feelings very plainly and soon Emma began to return them. Alexis was not strictly handsome, but his constantly changing expression, his dark piercing eyes with a twinkle in them, and his really charming smile were most attractive. He was something of a dandy, too, and his figure was set off to perfection by his broad-lapelled cutaway coat, with a froth of frilled cambric shirt at neck and wrist, and long slim lavender trousers which almost covered his lacquered boots. His silk cravat, maroon or black or plaid, was always arranged in the latest fashion— *l'Américaine*, *à la Byron*, *en Cascade*, or perhaps, when he was wooing Emma, *Sentimentale*. Fancy ran riot in waistcoats of flowered silk or shawl-patterned cashmere, while the heavy watch-chains, enormous scarf-pins and jewelled buttons which he loved were very much *à la mode* in 1837.

But no matter how splendid Soyer's clothes, how gallant his air, how witty his conversation, how charming his manner,

Simonau would not hear of bestowing the hand of his beloved Emma on a mere cook. Even so unusual a cook, with such excellent prospects, was still—a cook. Simonau produced instead an eligible young man of his own choice, who was always about the studio when Soyer came to sit for his portrait, and who tried to engage Emma's attention for himself. It was useless; she politely ignored him.

Alexis sent her verses extolling her talents:

> ...Terpsichore et Melpomène
> Me sont deux favoris!!
> Mais la peinture est l'art que j'aime,
> Emma elle seule je chéri...

and a long poem beginning:

> Ô vous, Emma, ô vous que mon cœur aime,
> Enfant gâté d'Apollon et des arts,
> Lorsque parfois, d'enthousiame extrême,
> Sur vos tableaux s'arrête mes regards,
> Mon âme ému ne peut en faire part;

each verse ending with a tribute to her 'beau talent' and an increasing number of exclamation marks. Whatever their merit as verses, Emma realised that these effusions expressed a real devotion, and received them kindly.

Alexis was the more horrified to receive, in return for a bouquet of tulips sent her, a very frigid card. 'Miss Jones is quite astounded at the liberty M. Soyer has taken in sending her such a present without her request, and consequently, by the next mail, he will receive a box and his flowers back; and it will be useless for him to send any more, as she will return them in the same manner.' Upset and disappointed, Alexis opened the box, and was astonished and delighted to find in it a charming painting of the flowers he had sent. It was the only thing needed to prove their affinity—she too could play a practical joke.

Despite Simonau's disapproval, they were married on 12th April 1837 at St George's, Hanover Square, Emma being

given away by Louis Eustache Ude, at that time the Grand
Old Man of London cooking.

When Soyer knew him, Ude was getting twelve hundred
pounds a year as steward and *maître d'hôtel* at Crockford's
Club, and lived with his wife in Albemarle Street. The house
was large, and the upper rooms were let to Lord Alvanley,
the witty spendthrift whom Greville thought 'the delight and
ornament of society', and O'Connell 'a bloated buffoon'.
Alvanley was not a model lodger, for he always read in bed,
and would never blow out his candle, but threw it into the
middle of the room and if it was still alight flung a pillow at
it. As fitted a lodger of Ude's, however, he was an extravagant
epicure; his favourite dish, a cold apricot tart, appeared on
his table daily throughout the year. He insisted that his
suprême de volaille should be made with the oysters of fowls
instead of the breasts, so that a moderate dish required a
score of fowls, and he once had a fricassée made with the
noix of three hundred birds, which is said to have cost him
one hundred and eight pounds.

Ude was very quick-tempered; he and his wife quarrelled
incessantly, and through the noise of their shrill scoldings
Alvanley would hear the barking of their five or six dogs and
the hoarse cries of their parrot, while at night the howls of
their cats were added to the din. Ude's exhibitions of temper
were not confined to his own home. He was found one day
marching up and down the hall of Crockford's in a towering
passion. A member had ordered a red mullet for dinner, and
Ude with his own hands had dressed it with a delicious sauce.
'The price on the *carte* for mullet', cried the *chef*, 'was two
shillings. I added sixpence for the sauce, and he refused to
pay it. The *imbécile* apparently believes that the red mullets
come out of the sea with my sauce in their pockets!'

Though avaricious—he died very rich—Ude every year
invited some twenty disciples and their wives to a birthday
feast on 25th August. Soyer's high spirits and quick wits, as

well as his rapid advancement in his profession, made him one of Ude's favourites, and one of his invitations survives:

> Dear Sir,
>
> You will oblidge me to favour with your Company you and your Wiffe, on Wednesday next at ½ past five o'clock been my birthday.
>
> Your truly, L. E. UDE.

On these occasions everyone wore his finest clothes, the gentlemen in broad-lapelled tight-waisted 'frocks' of maroon and blue, lace frilled shirts, flowered waistcoats, long tight pantaloons of rich cream silk and silk stockings with embroidered clocks. And their wives billowed gorgeously in their enormous sleeves, which made their waists seem tinier than ever, their white shoulders rising from muslins and nankin silks and chintzes and clouds of tulle caught up with rosebuds, while ostrich feathers nodded on turbans, toques and caps. Gold and silver plate shone on the table and the dishes were exquisitely chosen and cooked; fish, flesh, poultry, vegetables and fruit were each the best of its kind.

Almost always, however, the harmony of the feast was spoilt by the antics of Ude's dogs and cats, excited by the arrival of so many strangers. Years afterwards Soyer told the story of an unfortunate young man who trod on the paw of Madame's favourite dog, Vermillion. The dog bit him—he kicked out—several other dogs joined in—the host and hostess shouted through the din. It was an hour before calm was restored, and to everyone's disappointment the dinner, which had been one of the finest possible, was served up cold, entirely spoiled.

Each guest was expected to send a birthday gift in advance, and Emma one year sent a picture of a market-girl with a wicker basket of fowls on her head, which Ude prized highly, and refused to sell back to Soyer when he was collecting his wife's pictures after her death.

After her marriage Emma took up oil painting; she toured the provinces with Simonau, and several of her works were engraved and became very popular. From the age of eighteen until her death she exhibited at the British Institution and with the Society of British Artists at the Suffolk Street Gallery, while her first picture in the Royal Academy Exhibitions was hung in 1823, when she was only thirteen years old. She appeared regularly in the catalogue of Academy exhibitors from 1830 until her death, despite some quarrel with the President, Sir Martin Archer Shee, which led Soyer to write several rude verses 'Aux Royaux Académiciens'. He addressed them as 'Étoiles couvertes d'un obscur nuage', and one poem completed after his wife's death declares in a manner more bathetic than affecting,

> Elle vécue et morue en vraie chrétienne
> Sans désirer jamais devenir Académicienne.

The Times recorded that 'Madame Soyer was known among the less jealous of her fraternity as "the English Murillo"', and some idea of the nature of her art can be gathered from the titles of her paintings—'Children with Rabbits', 'The Little Masquerader', 'Willy and his Dog', 'A Chelsea Pensioner in his 104th Year', 'The Young Bavarian'—while she is described as specialising in 'Domestic' and 'Figure' studies. Horace Vernet said of 'The Young Bavarian' that 'no female artist had ever painted in such a *bold* style, nor with such truthfulness of colour and design'.

When Murillo's 'St John' was first shown in the National Gallery, Emma was offered a hundred guineas for an exact copy of it. This commission she refused, lest her other pictures should also be taken for mere copies of Murillo, but she engaged two handsome Italian boys as models, and promised to execute 'a Murillo of her own'. In a month's time she had completed 'The Young Savoyards Resting', described by the *Observer* as 'at once spiritedly and artistically executed'.

A companion piece of two boys selling lemons, called 'The Young Israelites', was so vigorous that a Mr Fitzgerald would not believe that a woman had painted it until he was

introduced to the artist. He asked her if she meant to paint
any more. Startled, she cried, 'Indeed, sir, I hope so!'
'Well,' he said, 'you are wrong; you will never excel this
picture. It is so true to nature that I might ask the little
urchins to take the lemons to my house.'

She loved to paint children with animals, white mice, dogs,
rabbits, and even donkeys and ponies. A Margate donkey
was carried every day up to her first-floor studio, while she
painted it with its master—'The Two Inseparables'. When
the picture was almost finished, the boy's mother came to see
it and, indignant because his knee showed through his ragged
trouser, carried off the model to dress him in his Sunday best.
The very old were often as difficult. The original of 'The
Centenarian Scotch Knitter' demanded heavy payment, refused to stop knitting, and insisted on being painted in her
own room, which was so tiny that Emma had to sit on the bed.

Her last portrait was of M. Pouchet, aged 107, a most
lively old man, 'never more offended than when asked to ride
in a cab', who had been leader of the orchestra at Drury Lane
some fifty years before. His favourite amusement was to walk
to Brompton to see his youngest son, who was, his father
loved to explain, 'infirm by reason of his great age'. Emma's
portrait was so striking that 'a certain Royal Duke' marched
up to the picture and exclaimed, 'I thought I heard my old
friend Pouchet had died, but I perceive he is still alive.'

In 1840 she exhibited 'The Centenarian' and 'The English
Ceres' at the Louvre. The latter was inspired by the sight of
a gleaner crossing a stubble field; Emma impulsively asked
her to pose, and the resulting picture was one of her most
admired feats. (Engravings of it, made some years after her
death, sold by the score.) The French critics were enthusiastic,
but thought 'Madame Soyer' must be a pseudonym; 'no
woman ever painted with so much vigour and ease', said *Le
Feuilleton du Capitol*. Her 'exquisite pieces' were praised for
'the correctness of drawing, the vigour, the manner, and the
purity of colouring' by *La Revue des Deux Mondes*, and she

was flatteringly mentioned in the *Revue Poétique du Salon de* 1840; her husband proudly added these panegyrics to his collection of Emma's tributes from the press.

She was not only a painter and musician of talent, but a clever housewife, and she somehow found time to act as her husband's secretary, writing all his correspondence and bills of fare.[1] An amusing little essay in sarcasm, *Fashionable Precepts for the Ladies*, survives as evidence of her wit:

Nothing [she wrote], in the eye of Fashion, is more amiable than to deviate from Nature.

To speak naturally, to act naturally, are vulgar and commonplace in the last degree. . . .

On any sudden alarm, either faint or fall into hysterics; perhaps the latter may be preferred as being the most fashionable, and as testifying the greatest emotion. But beware that in your attempts you do not bear a resemblance to a person labouring under the falling sickness, for this is a disorder as vulgar as hysterical convulsions are sentimental and polite. . . .

Study the art of blushing with peculiar interest, and let the crimson overspread your visage on every occasion where the empire of modesty is threatened with invasion. You should even wear flying colours for less occasions, and practice will give a facility in assuming this natural pigment, of which you have no conception.

Take your meals invariably later than your vulgar neighbours. Go to bed at two in the morning, and rise at twelve next day.

You will then become a fashionable lady, and, in the midst of congratulation, will entirely forget the sacrifice of truth and nature by which you have acquired this enviable distinction.

One of Emma's great gifts was her ability to catch a likeness in a few strokes. One day, tired of waiting for her husband in his room at the Reform Club, she sketched her own portrait on the wall, then rang the bell and told the porter she must go, but—pointing to the wall—had left her card. Soyer was delighted; he had a frame put round the sketch and a glass over it; many members heard the story and came down to see his latest exhibit. His room was already hung with her

[1] After her death Soyer took writing lessons to try to bring the menus up to their old standard of legibility.

paintings, and the visitors who thronged to see the kitchens were always shown Madame Soyer's pictures as well. One of the best ways to secure a superlative dinner was to be a great admirer of Madame Soyer's style.

In August 1842 the Duke of Saxe-Coburg was to visit his brother the King of the Belgians in Brussels. The duke had admired the kitchens of the club, and had been no less interested in Madame Soyer's paintings, so suggested that the *chef* should go with him and explain the one while exhibiting the other to the king. Emma was expecting a child quite soon, but she was so well that she urged Alexis to go, saying he needed a holiday.

On 29th August Madame Soyer was in her usual high spirits. She had a beautiful greyhound, and her servant happening to pick it up gracefully, Emma made a sketch of them as they stood, saying, 'I shall make a very pleasing picture of you both after my confinement'. The girl then asked if she might go to a new play, *Angels and Lucifers*. 'Nonsense!' said Emma, 'Why go to the theatre for that? We have plenty of lucifers here and I shall draw you lots of angels—won't that do for you?' She began idly sketching a design of her initials intertwined, with her palette surrounded by laurel. When the servant asked her what she was doing she said, 'Oh! it's only a bit of my nonsense', and put it away in a chiffonier. Soyer found it a month later and used the design on her tombstone.

As the day drew on the skies darkened, and in the evening a violent thunderstorm broke over London. Emma became terribly alarmed and upset. She was prematurely confined, and both she and the child died.

His friends did not dare to send Soyer the news by letter; they wrote only that Emma and the child were dangerously ill, and that he must prepare to return home at once. One of his friends, M. Volant, went to Brussels to break the news and bring him home.

Soyer met him by chance in the street as soon as he arrived, and hailed him with delight.

'What brings you here?'

'An errand which will let me travel home with you.'

'Did you see Emma before you left?'

'I did.'

'How is she?'

'Not so well as we hoped.'

'She is worse?'

'I fear so—'

They were moving along towards Soyer's lodging, Volant hoping to reach it before he had to tell his friend the truth. Suddenly Alexis turned on him and took his arm, 'For God's sake tell me—are you not the messenger of death? Is she dead?'

He saw in an instant that it was so; the sudden shock was like a physical blow. He shrank from the sympathy of Simonau's brother, his host, and his whole manner was so strange and wild that his friends feared for his reason. In his first frenzied grief he attempted to kill himself, and though he was calm enough to travel back to England the next day, the return to his empty home plunged him once more into deep melancholy.

Now for the first time Simonau and Soyer became really intimate. Simonau had always been devoted to his step-daughter, and since the death of her mother in 1839 all his affection had been concentrated on Emma. However great the artist's scorn of cooking as a profession, he had found it as difficult to resist Soyer's personal charm, as it was impossible not to be amused by his high spirits, and for the last few years they had been on excellent terms. Emma's death drew them closer together.

Soyer's former employer, the Marquis of Ailsa, invited them both to stay with him for a time, but a quiet holiday merely gave Alexis time to dwell on his loss; he soon came back to the club, and found his only relief in being overwhelmed with work.

He was proud of the appreciative obituaries of Emma that appeared in all the newspapers, and his greatest consolation was his work on a design for a monument to his wife. This was executed by M. Puyenbroach, and is a most remarkable erection, which became the talk of the town, and was for long the most conspicuous monument in Kensal Green Cemetery. 'It consists', says a contemporary account, 'of a colossal figure of Faith, with her right hand pointing towards Heaven; at her feet, lightly floating upon clouds, are two cherubim, the one holding a crown over the head of, and the other presenting a palm to, the deceased, who is represented on a beautiful medallion executed in white marble. A palette and brushes, embellished with a wreath of unfading laurel, is placed beneath the medallion.... The railing is cast most elaborately, from a design by Mr Rogers, the great artist in wood-carving.'[1]

There was a solemn unveiling ceremony, at which the famous danseuse Fanny Cerito (who will be heard of again) laid a wreath at the foot of the pedestal. This wreath was made from a crown of laurel which had been placed on her head by an Austrian archduke on the stage of La Scala at Milan, and it was preserved, with Madame Soyer's palette and brushes, under a glass panel at the back of the monument.

There had been much discussion and asking of advice about the inscription, Monckton Milnes suggesting the words 'Soyez tranquille', but much as Alexis rejoiced in a pun his real sorrow for once banished his jocularity. In contrast to all the elaboration of the monument, the inscription under Emma's name was simply 'To Her'; twelve years later he discovered that her married name made strangers suppose her a foreigner, and added a further legend—'England gave her birth; Genius immortality.'

Though only thirty-two when she died, Emma left over four hundred completed works. Her husband refused to sell any more of them, and tried to buy for himself as many as

[1] This wooden railing decayed, and was removed about 1930.

possible of those already sold. He hung them thickly upon the walls of his sanctum in the club, and those that could not be squeezed in there were first kept in the tiny flat he shared with Simonau, and afterwards went with him wherever he lodged.[1] They hung on walls and doors, were stacked in cupboards, piled in corners, and leant against the walls all round the rooms.

Nothing pleased him more than to show them off to visitors. He would take out his silk handkerchief and gently dust the surface of a picture, arrange it in the best light, and expatiate at length on its beauty and unique excellence, and on the various ways in which his wife had surpassed all other painters alive and dead. 'Ah!' he would say, 'I shall never marry again. I shall never find a woman like Emma. She shone as a painter, as a musician, as a housewife, and had a hundred other amiable qualities. What a treasure she was!'

[1] He was parted from them for the first time when he went to the Crimean war, and left them in the care of his old friends, Mr Crosse and Mr Blackwell. His two favourite pictures he took with him to the East, and kept beside him throughout the campaign.

CHAPTER III

CHEF DE CUISINE TO THE REFORM CLUB

'Then I came on deck and watched Moorshed...learned in experience withheld from me, moved by laws beyond my knowledge, authoritative, entirely adequate, and yet, in heart, a child at his play. *I* could not take ten steps along the crowded deck but I collided with some body or thing, but he and his satellites swung, passed and returned on their vocations with the freedom and spaciousness of the well-poised stars.'
KIPLING, *Traffics and Discoveries*

AFTER his wife's death Soyer's desire to be noticed, to be admired, above all to be extraordinary, grew ever more dominant. He tried not only to cook differently from everyone else, but to dress and talk and walk differently too. Brummel, it is said, ordered his gloves from two firms, one making the thumbs and the other the four fingers, and though Soyer never went to quite such lengths, yet he was a plague to his tailor, his hatter and his cravat-maker, for he would not wear a single garment with either horizontal or perpendicular lines. His hats were specially built so that when clapped on at any angle they slanted in a coquettish way—in his own phrase, *à la zoug-zoug*. His coats had to be cut on the cross, and as the years passed their cuffs grew deeper and deeper, their lapels ever larger and more flowing, and if his tailor ventured to modify these eccentricities, Soyer followed Lord Petersham's example and cut out the pattern himself. His visiting card (which said simply, 'Alexis Soyer, London, Paris' in exaggerated gothic lettering) was not a rectangle but a parallelogram; so was his cigar-case, and even the handle of his cane slanted obliquely.

His cravats were triumphs of ingenuity—folded in half a dozen ways, each more elaborate than the last—and his waistcoat might be of crimson gold-embroidered velvet, or (with a black dress coat) white satin worked with coloured silks. He was a true descendant of Cardinal Wolsey's Master Cook, 'who went daily in damask satin or velvet, with a chain of gold about his neck', for rings shone on Soyer's fingers, chains on his waistcoat and elaborate scarf-pins on his cravat. In the evening his glittering waistcoat buttons were set with turquoises and brilliants.

The French Romantic movement had almost run its course; women's clothes were declining into the sobriety of mid-Victorian respectability; men's clothing had already fallen from the glories of the 'twenties and 'thirties into the dull uniformity which was to possess it ever after. The elegant 'dandies' with their top boots and tasselled canes were becoming heavy 'swells', with top hats and full-skirted coats and Dundreary whiskers. Disraeli had had in 1830 a morning cane and an evening cane, changed punctually at noon; in 1828 he had appeared in 'green velvet trousers, a canary-coloured waistcoat, low shoes, silver buckles, and lace at his wrists'; in 1833 he had been hardly less gorgeous in 'a black velvet coat lined with satin, purple trousers with a gold band running down the outside seam, a scarlet waistcoat, long lace ruffles falling down to the tips of his fingers, and white gloves with several brilliant rings outside'; but by 1845 he was hardly distinguishable from any other M.P., dressing always in black, without either chains or rings.

But there was still Gautier, wearing always the red waistcoat he had worn for the first night of *Hernani*; there was still—until his creditors chased him out of England—the inimitably elegant Count D'Orsay, inventor of the paletot, whom tailors paid to patronise them, and who rode in tight leathers and polished boots, a blue coat with gilt buttons, a wide-brimmed glossy hat, and skin-tight white gloves; there was also Soyer, all *à la zoug-zoug*, refusing to dwindle into drab uniformity, and following no fashion but his own whim.

Thackeray, who frequented the Reform Club, was much entertained by the *chef*'s vagaries, and drew on Soyer's more fantastic and absurd affectations for Mirobolant, the French cook in *Pendennis*. This is definitely a caricature, and not a portrait; Mirobolant is a very silly fellow, and that was not the author's opinion of Soyer. Though Thackeray declared that the best chops in the world were to be had at the Reform Club, and once when he saw boiled bacon and beans (*à la Soyer*) on the club menu broke a dinner engagement to stay and dine on them, he did not admire Soyer merely as a cook. 'Thackeray', wrote George Augustus Sala, who knew them both, 'had towards Soyer the friendliest feelings, and genuine admiration to boot; since the mercurial Frenchman was something more than an excellent cook—that is to say, Alexis was a man of sound commonsense, a practical organiser, a racy humorist and a constant sayer of good things.'

'A constant sayer of good things'—a very pleasant epitaph, but jokes made in company are of all things the most evanescent, and have the highest rate of mortality. Read a verbatim record of the wittiest gathering; each jest seems as pointless as the empty case of an exploded firework. There is abundant testimony to the high opinion of Soyer's wit held by his contemporaries. 'He was never half-an-hour in a place', wrote one of them, 'before the laughter would cause the enquiry of "What's the matter?" or "Who's there?" "Why, that's Soyer", would be the response.' It is said that even needle-sharp Douglas Jerrold met his match for quickness in Soyer.[1]

Perhaps the *chef*'s broken English gave his jokes added value, for in most recorded conversations he is made to replace *th* by *d*—'dere' for 'there', and so on, like a nigger minstrel. It may be that his ever-present desire to be different made him exaggerate the eccentricity of his pronunciation, for even after twenty-five years in England his accent was

---

[1] Soyer never forgave Jerrold for saying that the sorrow expressed in Emma's monument was 'mock turtle'.

almost as marked as on his first arrival. He had, all the same, an excellent knowledge of the language, and puns were his forte. Lord Melbourne, when being shown round the kitchens, remarked on the prettiness of the young women cooks. 'My lord,' said Soyer at once, 'we do not want plain cooks here.'

Most of Soyer's jokes were so spontaneous and good-natured that even the victims were amused. Holding forth one afternoon to a stranger he had met in a Haymarket restaurant, Soyer began to abuse the 'friends of liberty' who had set up the new Republic of 1848 in France. He declared that they had destroyed all beauty and elegance, and that now 'the white inexpressibles of the National Guard were exposed to dry at every window of the Palace of the Tuileries, giving to that noble building somewhat the appearance of a Rag Fair'. The unknown happened to be an officer of the French navy named Cournet, a celebrated duellist, and these last remarks infuriated him. He called Soyer a monarchist and an enemy of liberty, and insisted that they should meet the next morning, to give each other the satisfaction due from gentlemen. Soyer must tell the rest himself.

'I replied to his challenge by desiring that the matter should be settled at once.

'He answered in a haughty tone, "Comme vous voudrez, monsieur. C'est à vous le choix des armes. Nous tirerons ce que vous voudrez!"

'"Eh bien," said I, "puisque c'est à moi le choix des armes, sortons à l'instant même, monsieur, et nous allons tirer les cheveux."'[1]

A roar of laughter from everyone around blew away the quarrel, and Soyer explained to Cournet that his mission 'was to make people live well, not to make them die badly'.

[1] To show that he was not confined to one language, Soyer himself translated the joke: '"As you please, sir, the choice of weapon is yours."—"In that case I suppose we must pull triggers for it."—"Sir," replied he, "we will pull any mortal thing you like!"—"Good," said I, "then we will pull one another's hair."'

His practical jokes are less pleasing,[1] but allowance must be made for the fashion of the time. (Did not the first gentleman of the land slip an ice down Mrs Langtry's décolletage?) And some of them are amusing enough. One night he appeared at the door of Her Majesty's in morning dress, and was refused admittance. 'Why?' asked Soyer. 'Because—' began the commissionaire, then looking again at the *chef* he rubbed his eyes—Soyer was now in full evening dress! He had contrived a trick suit which changed its style when he pulled a string.[2]

One snowy night in 1849, Soyer was sitting chatting in a favourite haunt, 'Frost's' in Bow Street. A friend came in with two fowls which he had bought to take home. Soyer manœuvred the party into another room, then seized the fowls and vanished below into the kitchens. When he reappeared he invited his friend to wait and share some supper he had ordered. The friend demurred—he had already supped at Jacquet's alamode-beef-house—but was eventually persuaded to stay. Presently ten people sat down to a delicious fricassée of fowl. The unfortunate victim never dreamt that he had supplied the dish, but praised it highly and ordered brandy all round as a 'settler'.[3] When he was heartily thanked by the company, not only for the brandy, but for the fowls too, he was—very naturally—furious, and swore he would never trust Soyer again. But the others went home in such high spirits that they tumbled each other in the snow, reeling along helpless with laughter.

Soyer's early love for the stage was as strong as ever, and he was on the free list of every theatre in London. Talking with his friends in the evening, he would suddenly ask what was being played at Drury Lane, or Her Majesty's. 'What?

---

[1] See pp. 125, 157–8.

[2] Cf. Aby Gussow, of Brooklyn, who invented a night-shirt which by pulling a switch turned into a pair of pyjamas. Reported in the *Daily Express*, 4th January 1938.

[3] This cost him half-a-crown for ten people.

Lucrezia Borgia, and Cerito in the ballet? I shall certainly
go.' Half an hour later he would stroll into the foyer, in full
evening dress—blue tail coat with gilt buttons, black trousers,
satin waistcoat with gold sprigs, shirt abundantly frilled—
drawing on his elegant white kid gloves, chatting with
Captain This or Colonel That, or escorting some pretty
woman. He was one of the most regular frequenters of the
'Fops' Alley' at Her Majesty's, where all the dandies
gathered. He knew everybody. 'Go where he would,' wrote
a friend, 'either in his own world the cuisine, the literary or
theatrical world, the fashionable world, or into *purlieus* which
out of mere curiosity he sought to know, everybody liked
him.'

The evening was often wound up with supper at the
'Provence' or the 'Albion' or some other popular eating-
house. Soyer's appearance was hailed with shouts of delight,
and after supper there were always calls for a song. Everyone
liked his most frequent *chansonnette*:

> Vive le militaire!
> Pour séduire un tendron,
> En amour comme en guerre,
>   Le militaire
> Est toujours bon luron.
>
> Où va, donc, Seulette,
> Disait un beau troupier,
> À la gentille Annette,
> Qu'il voyait cheminer.
> Permets que je t'accompagne,
> Ne fais pas de façon,
> F'sons un tour de campagne,
> Viens—j'ai ma permission.

Then the whole company would join in the chorus, 'Vive le
militaire'. In answer to the cries of 'Encore', and shouts of
applause, Alexis would call out, 'Ah, my boys, you are all
good friends to me. I *nevare* can return your compliments!'
and then oblige with another song.

He saw a good deal of his friend from Wales, Charles Pierce, and they both became intimate with the remarkable Yorkshire stable-boy Tom Ward, who became Baron Ward and Prime Minister of the Duchy of Parma. Ward corresponded with Pierce all his life, and in one of his last letters said that he hoped soon to be in London again, 'to see his merry friend Soyer, and enjoy an hour of his conversation.'

No amount of fame or responsibility seemed to repress Soyer's love of fooling. Being invited to a party given by one of the Queen's cooks at Windsor, he set out with a friend nicknamed Briolet, known as a wit, a dancer, and a singer of comic songs. As they left the coach a heavy shower began; Briolet hastily pulled the wrapper off Soyer's umbrella, and though at the top of it there was a hole eighteen inches across, they solemnly held it over them as they marched through Windsor, ignoring equally the rain splashing through the hole, the laughter of passers-by, and the jeering of the little boys who ran hooting after them.

The dinner was magnificent, and was to be followed by a ball the next day. Wandering round Windsor in the morning, the two friends met a Frenchman who was having trouble with an inadequate and ignorant guide, and they offered to help him.

'You are very kind...my interpreter knows less than I do...I have so little time to see Windsor....'

'Don't worry,' said Soyer, 'we will show you *everything*.'

The Frenchman turned out to be 'M. Ernest Bourdin, Bookseller and Publisher, Captain of the National Mounted Guard, Paris.' He seemed an excellent fellow, so Soyer immediately introduced Bourdin to his own host, and after a whirlwind tour of the castle, insisted on taking him on to the ball.

'At that time', said a fellow-guest, 'most of the artist-cooks, confectioners and pastry-cooks in her Majesty's service were married or about to be married to very pretty women. As the company consisted mostly of foreigners there was a kind of freedom and gaiety which made the whole party exceedingly happy.' Bourdin was in ecstasies. 'It is not possible! It is a dream! Am I at Windsor? No, it cannot be! Those French faces, those pretty women! I shall never forget this meeting! Only give me a chance to show how grateful I am.'

In fact, the hospitable gesture was repaid the following spring, when Bourdin introduced Soyer's first book, *Délassements Culinaires*, to Paris, and to M. Fayot, editor of *Les Classiques de la Table*.

In 1846 Soyer became friendly with Philippe, a French conjuror who unfortunately did not confine his conjuring to the stage. The railway mania was then in full swing, and he speculated in railway shares, persuading Soyer to join him. When settling day came Philippe did a vanishing trick, leaving Soyer to settle with their creditors.

He lost over a thousand pounds, but still refused to think ill of his friend; the imperfect syntax of the letter he sent to Philippe does not hide his affection and optimism. 'You are', writes Soyer, 'a naughty fellow.... Notwithstanding the misfortune weighing heavily upon us—more particularly me, because I never had a wish to speculate in anything, being satisfied with the produce of my humble talent, whilst on the other hand you are a sublime genius, perhaps a little too exalted, leading you to heavenly dreams whose time has not yet arrived—I hope that we shall live and love each other for a long time to come on this earth.... N'importe what may happen, be always Philippe, and I swear on my honour that Soyer shall always remain Soyer.... London is full of people, advertise well, and Christmas will put us on our legs again.'

During the eighteen-forties the kitchens of the Reform Club became celebrated as the epitome of gastronomic perfection. *Punch*, for instance, scoffing at an advertisement requiring 'cooks' for the Stepney Union, enquires if the union has kitchens like those of the Reform Club, to need not 'a cook' but 'cooks'; the *Spectator* eulogises the 'matchless culinary arrangements of the Reform Club', and there are countless other references. Their fame was not confined to England, and an account of them by the Viscountess de Malleville appeared in the *Courrier de l'Europe*.

'The kitchen', she writes, 'is spacious as a ballroom, kept in the finest order, and white as a young bride.' She marvels at the many uses to which steam is put—warming plates, keeping dishes hot, turning the spits, drawing water and carrying coal. 'Around you', she goes on, 'the water boils and the stewpans bubble, and a little farther on is a movable furnace, before which pieces of meat are transformed into savoury *rôtis*—here are sauces and gravies, stews, broths, soups, etc.; in the distance are Dutch ovens, marble mortars, lighted stoves, iced plates of metal for fish, and various compartments for vegetables, fruits, roots and spices.... The reader may perhaps picture to himself a state of general confusion...if so, he is mistaken, for in fact you see very little of all the objects above described; the order of their arrangement is so perfect, their distribution as a whole, and in their relative bearings to one another, all are so intelligently considered, that you require the aid of a guide to direct you in exploring them, and a good deal of time to classify in your mind all your discoveries.'

She declares that the cleanliness of the smallest recesses would shame many a drawing-room, and after an appreciation of Soyer, creator of all this splendour and presiding genius, she exhorts all visitors to London to visit the Reform Club. 'In an age of utilitarianism, and of the search for the comfortable, like ours, there is more to be learnt here than in the ruins of the Coliseum, of the Parthenon, or of Memphis.'

A 'lithographic view' of the kitchens was prepared, which showed the whole basement of the building with the partition walls cut away, exposing the arrangement of all the kitchens, larders and sculleries. Various cooks and kitchenmaids and waiters were shown at their work, and in the centre was the

The kitchens of

chef himself, proudly showing two fashionable visitors the glories of his kingdom. This print, three feet by one, was very popular, and fourteen hundred copies of it were sold, at a guinea coloured and half a guinea plain.

Towards the end of the 'forties, sightseers became so numerous that Soyer's secretary was continually called away from his real work to be polite to Lord This or Count That, who came with letters of introduction, and wanted to see the culinary arrangements, and if possible to meet the *chef*. From twelve till four there was a constant stream of visitors, some wishing to see the kitchens, some to see Emma's paintings, some to meet Soyer in person, to ask him to suggest a menu, or recommend a cook, or merely to pass the time of day.

Some of the epicurean members used to shake him heartily by the hand, and enquire about his health. 'These had', he wrote some years later, 'a twofold object in view, first, to induce me to give them the best of dinners; secondly, to ascertain whether I was feverish or in good health. In the

former case they would postpone their dinner-party for a few days, or else try to persuade me to follow the plan of the celebrated Marquis de Coucy...who never engaged a cook without having a written agreement, giving him power to compel his cook to take a purge [to ensure a clean palate] a couple of days before he gave any of his grand dinners, which never exceeded twelve in the Paris season.' This was, of course, the plan recommended by Grimod de la Reynière, but whether many epicures actually practised it is perhaps doubtful.

Specially distinguished visitors were shown round by Alexis himself, resplendent in shining white apron, with his red velvet cap perched over one ear, waving a long spoon as a pointer. He enjoyed nothing better than explaining to noble lords and elegant ladies the composition of a soup, or the flavouring of a sauce, and would tempt his visitors with a spoonful of delicious mulligatawny, or a mouthful of *Pâté de Volaille aux Truffes*, sending them away ravenous. Sometimes, his secretary wrote, 'he would plunge his finger, diamond ring and all, into what appeared to be a boiling cauldron of glue, pass it across his tongue, wink his eye, and add either a little more salt, pepper, or some mysterious dust, known only to great artistes, to make it palatable. Or he would whisper, chucklingly, "I've a dish for Lord M— H— for six o'clock, or a potage for Sir J— So-and-so at eight o'clock; let us taste it!"'

In theory he rested for an hour at four o'clock, but in practice the first crowd of visitors seldom left much before five, when a fresh stream began. At five he went into the kitchens, and moved about supervising everything, now and then making a sauce or dressing a dish for some favoured gourmet with his own hands. He was often still surrounded by acquaintances, and kept up a continual stream of puns and jests, while all the time the clerk of the kitchen called for the various dinners as they were required, and Soyer saw that each dish went up at the right moment and in perfect condition.

Even on the busiest evenings he found time to ask the clerk how much money the day's work would bring in. Careless and even reckless with his own money, Soyer was scrupulously exact with that of other people, and it was his pride and delight to make the extravagance of the members pay for the servants' meals. He was often able to tell the committee that the sixty or seventy servants had been well fed for a week at four or five shillings a head.

When the last dish had been sent up he would fling away his cap and apron, and, still surrounded by friends, change hastily into full dress. Then off they would go to concert, theatre or opera, Soyer rarely bothering to wait and eat his own supper. If hungry later he would send out for a quart jug of Jacquet's alamode beef, or go to an eating-house, or dive into any little shop that sold bread and cheese. More than once he was met walking along eating with the greatest enjoyment twopenny worth of fried fish from a paper bag. No matter how humble their table, none of Soyer's friends hesitated to ask him to share a meal. On one occasion when dining out he expressed great admiration for the curried rabbit, refused other dishes, swore he had never tasted it so well done, asked for the receipt, and had three helpings of it. There was much laughter when the host declared it was cooked from a receipt invented by one Soyer.

As if his multifarious duties and responsibilities were not enough to occupy his mind, Alexis was constantly inventing one thing or another; some of these inventions are described in a later chapter. They ranged from a contrivance for keeping money in the heels of his dress boots to an immense new roasting-range for the club kitchens, which saved two hundredweight of coal a day, and needed no poking. It was so effectively screened, he said, that 'I have many times placed ladies and gentlemen visiting the club within two feet of the fire when six large joints have been roasting, and they have been in perfect ignorance that it was near them until upon opening the wing of the screen by surprise, they have appeared quite terrified to think they were so near such an immense furnace.'[1] Soyer's private room at the club, as well as being crowded with Emma's paintings, was always littered with gadgets of various kinds, the very latest invention being displayed on a special table in the window.

In this sanctum, sometimes, after the members' dinners were over, a few select friends would gather. Soyer would unlock his precious cupboard, filled with rare wines and liqueurs and brandies and spices and sauces; while his friends sat round with their mouths watering, he would create, with a spoonful of this, a pinch of that, and a soupçon of the other a dish fit for Apicius himself. His friends would taste it, gaze at him admiringly, taste again, and (as one of them deplorably expressed it) toast him as 'never a traitor, but most assuredly a *traiteur* of the class A 1'.

[1] This range was still in use eighty years after its installation, and a visitor seeing a single leg of mutton roasting before that immense fire, commented on the price each slice of mutton must cost the club.

Such suppers occasionally caused trouble. Some servant, jealous of the *chef*'s airs and the freedom allowed him, would report him to the committee. But Soyer, the picture of injured innocence, would invariably be able to produce vouchers showing that the only expense suffered by the club was the borrowing of its plate and glass—the ingredients for the suppers were paid for by himself. The chairman of the committee, Lord Marcus Hill, was his staunch supporter, and Soyer always defended himself with such vigour and wit that the affair would end with the committee breaking into laughter and the victorious exit of the triumphant *chef*.

From time to time there was a more serious disagreement. 'At times', says a historian of the club, 'he failed in respect towards his superiors'; in 1844 Soyer's resignation was accepted owing to his 'great irregularity'—he had in fact tried to seduce a kitchenmaid. But three days later he was reinstated, 'with full authority and powers over the whole kitchen staff'. His behaviour was already 'news'. Newspapers noticed the resignation, and a few days later the statement was published that 'M. Soyer remains at the Reform Club with the confidence of the members, if possible, increased.'

Everything to do with every department of the club interested Soyer, and he often got into hot water by his insistence not only on his own rights and privileges, but on those of other servants also, and by his interference with the general running of the club; if any servant got into trouble, the *chef* would hasten to defend him.

When the new club had been opened in March 1841, the members had had a grand opening dinner, but the servants had not had any particular celebration. Soyer proposed to the committee that in place of the quiet little dance which the servants always held at Christmas, there should this year be a grand ball, to which they might invite their friends. Though some members thought that to permit this was to go absurdly far in 'reformed' treatment of underlings, the committee agreed to the proposal, and arranged that the ball should be held in the banqueting-room. 'For a week previous', wrote one of the *chef*'s secretaries, 'the female portion of the servants could hardly be kept to their duties, so anxious were they to prepare their dresses for the ball.'

On Twelfth Night 1842 the members withdrew from the club; the banqueting-room was specially decorated, an excellent band had been engaged, and the supper was prepared *à la Soyer*. The whole affair was so unprecedented that some of the members' wives persuaded their husbands to bring them to the club for a few moments in the evening, to peep at the festivities. All went very well, and the party ended with cheers for its proposer.

Whatever Soyer did, he did with all his might; 'when he had once started anything,' wrote a friend, 'he hardly seemed to sleep till it was done, he was incredibly zealous and persevering in his cause', and even his superabundant energy could not survive this life of hard work and harder play, late hours and snatched meals. He began to feel listless and tired, and as both his brothers had died young, one of them of consumption, his friends grew alarmed. The doctor he consulted recommended a course of gymnastics, so various pieces of apparatus were put up in Soyer's rooms, and he began to exercise with his usual whole-heartedness. Soon his chest expanded, his health improved, and he felt himself again; but from this time he began to put on flesh, and to become the traditional figure of a cook.

Comedy or tragedy, melodrama or farce, even pantomime, Soyer enjoyed and applauded them all. Still better he loved opera and ballet, and he was one of the greatest enthusiasts among the balletomanes who thronged Her Majesty's Theatre during the early eighteen-forties. Ballet was all the rage; Taglioni was paid a hundred and twenty pounds a night, and devotees eagerly bought plaster models of Vestris's legs.

The manager, Mr Lumley, presented an astonishingly brilliant series of ballets, the most famous perhaps being the

Pas de Quatre, in which Taglioni, Carlotta Grisi, Cerito and Grahn actually appeared together. This was an immense sensation; never before had four great ballerinas consented to forego their individual triumphs and perform a concerted work.[1]

Soyer became an ardent admirer of charming Fanny Cerito, whose joyous abandon, brilliant twirling steps and wonderful revolving bounds contrasted so strikingly with Taglioni's flowing grace and precision of line. The spiritual quality of all Taglioni's movements, her rare elevation, and her aloof beauty, were less to Soyer's baroque taste than Cerito's flying leaps, her 'innocent playfulness', her 'voluptuous poses', her figure, which as a contemporary put it, 'would be too redundant were it not for its extreme flexibility and abandon'. She was one of the few women dancers who have attempted choreography. She collaborated with Perrot in *Alma* and *Ondine*, in each of which she danced the title-role, and also created several ballets herself. Cerito revolving brilliantly in *Alma*, Cerito dancing the famous 'Pas de l'Ombre' to her shadow in *Ondine*, Cerito 'twirling herself into supreme eminence' in the *Jugement de Paris*, 'coquetting and tantalising' in *Rosida*, dancing her 'captivating Redowa' or her 'admired pas de deux from *Les Houries*' with M. St Leon,[2] or her minuet with Ellsler, drew the town to Her Majesty's.

Cerito was a young woman of temper as well as temperament, and was very jealous of any fancied slight. She once returned the ticket of a box which had been given her on an upper tier, saying that she was 'much too young to be exalted to the stars before her proper time'. M. Laporte, then manager, had given Taglioni a box on the same tier, and

---

[1] There was great dispute as to precedence; it was agreed that Taglioni should have the fourth place, but each of the others insisted that she should dance third. Lumley suggested that they should dance in order of age, and at once each was willing to dance before the other two.

[2] Later she married M. St Leon, who was a violinist as well as a dancer, and sometimes performed violin solos between ballets.

replied that he 'had done his best, but that possibly he had
been wrong to put the lady on the same level [le même rang]
as Mademoiselle Taglioni'. But when other artists quarrelled,
Cerito was said to have 'the power of calming down all the
contending elements by one *rond de jambes*'.

Dish created in Cerito's honour

Her fame was European. The Prince of Salerno sent her
magnificent jewels; an Austrian archduke crowned her with
laurels; La Scala at Milan was opened out of season so that
she might dance there; Queen Adelaide sent her a brooch;
Soyer in his turn expressed his admiration by dedicating to

Cerito his airiest dishes, and by designing a 'Silver Terpsi-chorean Attelette' surmounted by a dancer, to crown these confections.

He persuaded her to sit to Simonau for her portrait, which he liked so well that he had it lithographed at his own expense. While she was being painted Soyer haunted the studio, and paid her every attention. But Père Cerito did not approve. He was his daughter's constant companion, and identified himself with her in all her doings—after one of her successes he would say, for instance, '*Nous* avons dansé magnifiquement ce soir.' To remove Fanny from Alexis's reach she was taken to Brighton.

Alexis was devoted enough to follow her there with various gifts, but when her mother definitely refused to consider his advances, he was not unduly depressed. His feelings for her were aesthetic rather than erotic, and after a consoling jollification with some Brighton friends he returned to London in his usual high spirits.

CHAPTER IV

'THE GASTRONOMIC REGENERATOR'

'All sensible and well-informed people know that cookery books are delightful reading; and most wholesome when perused for a short time before dressing for dinner, except in the case of the bad-blooded, who may be tempted to quarrel with the dinner itself in comparison.'

SAINTSBURY

IN 1845 Soyer published his first book, *Délassements Culinaires* —'Culinary Recreations'—a slim brochure elaborately printed in blue, each page ornamented with a fancy border. Typical of the author's eccentricity was the frontispiece, an elongated picture of Soyer's head as it might appear in a distorting mirror, which inspired a friend to write:

> Behold this phiz of awful length,
> Equipped with brain of wondrous strength,
> Compared with which Carême's were dull
> And Ude can scarcely boast a skull.
> Long-headed Soyer, may thy name
> Be *stretched* upon the rolls of Fame.

The *pièce de résistance* of the work is a ballet dedicated to Cerito. First there is an imaginary discussion between 'Mdlle C' and her friends, on the difficulty of composing an original ballet, since all possible subjects and scenes have already been used. An 'Amateur'—Soyer—declares that he will give her a new name, 'La Fille de l'Orage', and is challenged to produce an entire ballet with that title. The first act of the ballet is then detailed. *Bell's Life*, the famous sporting paper, when reviewing the book, thought that Soyer, 'confessedly one of the first of cooks... shows himself almost as much an artist in the production of ballets as of epicurean dishes'. But *La Fille de l'Orage* was indeed, as another critic described it, 'replete with choreographic difficulties', and though music was written for it some thirteen years later, it can hardly have been performed.

The essay goes on to imagine its reception; merely to read it moves Cerito to tears—of laughter. On the first night, despite the loveliness of 'la sémillante et séduisante Cerito, qui a vraiment dansé aussi légèrement qu'une gazelle qui folichonne une polka sur des rognures de fer blanc ou des allumettes chimiques', the audience bursts into cat-calls. The author, his face long and dismal as the book's frontispiece, is carried off to Bedlam.

Soyer's ballet is, in fact, a superb skit on the elaborate *ballet d'action*, then highly popular, though ten years later the swells were to declare it 'something that no fellow could understand', and refuse to attend anything but a *divertissement*. Here is a résumé of the first act. The setting is most minutely described: on the left a village (naturally 'extrêmement pittoresque'), lying at the foot of a mountain ('très riante et d'une fertilité remarquable') which is crowned with an ancient castle; on the right a gothic church ('un peu en ruines'), surrounded by various little houses and shrubs and trees; in the distance, many mountains, a marshy lake winding like a serpent between them.

The scenario demands continual complicated 'effects'. At first, joyful peasants are dancing while the sun sets in splendour behind the mountains, and the hero, Urbin, performs a 'pas seul'. Then a storm breaks, with clouds, thunder, lightning and rain, and the stage is in darkness relieved only by the lighted windows of houses and church. The hero is struck by lightning, and a house bursts into flames, while a cloud descends on the stage. When it clears, 'La Fille de l'Orage', daughter of Jupiter, is disclosed bending over the lifeless hero. She prays to Jupiter to restore him, then to Cupid; many baby Cupids with flaming torches 'appear to rise from the ground like flowers of love', and while she dances 'un pas de désespoir' they revive Urbin.

Now is the ballerina's great moment. 'Elle passe de la désolation au plaisir le plus vif, qu'elle exprime par un pas très remarquable.' The storm 'gronde au loin d'une manière effroyable'—Jupiter's reminder that she is divine—and she flies from Urbin, who pursues her hotly. The villagers, who are attempting to put out the burning house, are horrified, and the young girls try to catch Urbin and draw him back. In vain; the jealous goddèss encloses him in the cloud which Jupiter has sent to carry her home. 'Le vent d'une manière très gracieuse enlève le nuage, qui doucement côtoie la verte montagne.' The wretched producer is now called upon for another transformation scene. Rays of moonlight strike through the cloud, showing now and then a glimpse of Urbin kneeling at the feet of 'sa celeste madone'. The cloud vanishes among the rocks, but reappears for a moment in splendour above the mountain, leaving the villagers—and surely the audience—dumb and motionless with astonishment.

The other essays in the book are slight enough—strewn with puns and not very funny now that they are ninety years old. There is, too, a detailed description of the genesis of a new entrée dish,[1] and, finally, Soyer's receipt for *La Crème de la Grande Bretagne*. To compose this 'unparalleled receipt', in the words of *Blackwood's Magazine*, the author had need of 'the deepest erudition and the keenest ingenuity, the most delicate wit and the most outrageous folly'. It is compounded of such things as a Smile from the Duchess of Sutherland, a Mite of Gold from Miss Coutts, a Figment of the Work of Lady Blessington, a Ministerial Secret from Lady Peel; it is seasoned with such condiments as the Piquante Observations of the Marchioness of Londonderry, flavoured with such delicacies as the Innocent Trick of the Princess Royal, and mixed in the Cup of Hebe. This is covered with the reign of Her Most Gracious Majesty, and the brew is simmered for half a century over a Fire of Immortal Roses. And so on at great length—at much too great a length—though contem-

[1] The pagodatique entrée dish; see p. 63.

poraries admired the skill with which 'the ingenious *chef* blended together poetry, pastry and politics', and another edition of the book was printed.

In France too, this 'spirituelle et élégante brochure, dictée par un esprit si gracieux, une imagination si riche', was much admired. M. Fayot, editor of *Les Classiques de la Table*, well qualified to judge a gastronomic essay—'J'ai été l'ami de Carême pendant de longues années, celui du Marquis de Cussy [Coucy], de Grimod de la Reynière; j'ai connu Brillat-Savarin'—approved. 'Chez vous, monsieur,' he wrote to Soyer, 'le cuisinier rempli de goût et d'une charmante élégance, étincelle dans l'écrivain.'

On the very last page of *Délassements Culinaires* the reader is promised another work by the same author, a work on a very different scale, a work which was to set the seal on his reputation and give him his nickname, *The Gastronomic Regenerator*. It appeared in 1846, and was an instantaneous success. Two thousand copies at a guinea each were sold in a few months; in less than a year a fourth edition was called for; a sixth came out in 1849 and yet another in 1852, and to each new edition fresh essays and plates and embellishments were added by the indefatigable author.

The absurd but amusing preface explains the origin of the book, undertaken 'at the request of several persons of distinction—particularly the ladies, to whom I have always made it a rule never to refuse anything in my power.' But for years he had not been able to think of composing a cookery book without recalling with horror a day spent 'in a most superb library in the midst of a splendid baronial hall'. 'By chance,' he writes, 'I met with one of Milton's allegorical works, the profound ideas of Locke, and several *chefs-d'œuvre* of one of the noblest champions of literature, Shakespeare; when all at once my attention was attracted by the nineteenth edition of a voluminous work: such an immense success of publication caused me to say, "Oh! you celebrated man, posterity counts every hour of fame upon your regretted ashes!" Opening this work with intense curiosity, to my great disappointment what did I see—a receipt for Ox-tail Soup! The terrifying effect produced upon me by this succulent volume made me determine that my few ideas, whether culinary or domestic, should never encumber a sanctuary which should be entirely devoted to works worthy of a place in the Temple of the Muses.' But after much persuasion he has consented to compile the *Gastronomic Regenerator* and he begs his readers to keep it in the kitchen, 'and not with Milton's sublime Paradise, for there it certainly would be doubly lost'.

He explains that he has tried to be worthy of his title, and has 'closely studied to introduce the greatest novelty in every department' and—a striking innovation, as all who have studied earlier works on cooking must agree—he has 'entirely omitted all unnecessary confusion'.

The book was on such a scale—it contained two thousand receipts—that its production in less than ten months was a tremendous feat. As *The Times* reviewer put it, 'For ten months he laboured at the pyramid which the remotest posterity shall applaud; and during the whole of that period he was intent upon providing the countless meals which a living generation have already approved and fully digested. Talk of the labours of a Prime Minister or Lord Chancellor! Sir R. Peel was not an idle man. Lord Brougham was a tolerably busy one. Could either, we ask, in the short space of ten months...have written the *Gastronomic Regenerator*, and furnished 25,000 dinners, 38 banquets of importance, comprising above 70,000 dishes, besides providing daily for sixty servants, and receiving the visits of 15,000 strangers, all too eager to inspect the renowned altar of a great Apician temple? All this did M. Soyer.'

The book was, in fact, built up like one of his great dishes; his first kitchenmaid (who had been with him some years) and his first apprentice prepared the ingredients—that is, wrote down the methods and receipts—and the *chef* himself revised, unified, arranged and garnished the whole. On every page traces of the master's hand are discernible—an anecdote, a jest, or sometimes merely a sentence as forceful and expressive as it is ungrammatical. 'I have invented...', 'Those numerous innovations', 'still greater novelties...', such phrases occur again and again, with such remarks as 'This is quite a new idea, it not only looks well but likewise cuts and eats beautiful.'

It is said that G. K. Chesterton, when composing a play for his friends, did not write a song for the troubadour, explaining in surprise when asked for it that he had thought that the actor would much prefer to write his own. Soyer had in common with G. K. C. not only extravagant powers of invention, but much gusto and good humour and love of song, and he too could not understand why everyone did not enjoy creating. 'I consider it a pity', he writes, 'so few people make any experiments in cookery, which like other arts is almost inexhaustible.' Again, after giving precise directions for decorating a dish, he adds, 'But galantines may be ornamented in several elegant ways, entirely depending upon the taste of the individual', and it is obvious that he expects each cook to scorn imitation, and to make his own designs.

The main body of the *Gastronomic Regenerator* is divided into two parts, a long one on the 'Kitchen of the Wealthy', and a much shorter section on the 'Kitchen at Home'. The latter is full of sound, fairly simple and inexpensive receipts, very lucidly set out, and it might still be profitably used by the ordinary middle-class family. Even in this section novelties had to be introduced, and it is here that Soyer mentions what is surely one of the most remarkable of his inventions—nothing less than a new joint, called saddleback of mutton. 'This joint looks very noble, and does not appear too large when roasted', he says, but those who require something smaller are not forgotten—for them he suggests a new chop, and supplies an engraving to show the butcher how to cut it. General directions, and discussion of general principles—such as 'A few things I object to, that is, not to use in cookery comestibles when out of, or before, their proper season'—are meant for every class of cook.

Armed with these hints, and with the more elaborate receipts and instructions for the 'Kitchen of the Wealthy', a *chef* could produce every possible meal required for a large establishment, from comparatively simple though exquisite suppers to banquets graced with the most extravagant creations—*truffes de Périgord* (at four guineas a bottle) stewed in champagne; real roast peacocks dressed with tulips and roses, and mock peacocks made of sweetmeats, with sliced pistachios for neck feathers; boar's head *à l'Antique*, with orange in mouth, and boar's head *à la Soyer*, carved from sponge-cake, masked with chocolate icing, tusked with gum paste, eared with puff pastry, with fierce cherry eyes peering from beneath pistachio eyelashes; even a Chinese pagoda of meringue, complete with bells.

These, however, are mere frivolities and fantasies for special occasions; 'although the eye must be pleased to a certain extent,' writes Soyer, 'my principal business is with the palate'; and again, 'it is against my principle to have any unnecessary ornamental work in a dinner'. He admits, for instance, that ox-tails do not make handsome *entrées*, 'but their delicate flavour supplies their deficiency in appearance'.

Precise distinctions are made; only in veal can France surpass England when supplying meat, but all English meat is not equally good—as to Leicestershire mutton, 'I consider it more as a useful nourishment than a delicate meat'. Again, gurnets are ranked as 'one of the first of the second-class fishes'.

Every department of cookery is dealt with in turn—sauces, soups, fish, hors d'œuvres, removes for the first course, flancs, entrées, savouries, vegetables (and their garnitures), entremets, removes for the second course,[1] soufflés and preserves.

[1] The two classes of removes are differentiated, for 'what would look noble in the first course would appear vulgar in the second'.

Each section has a miniature preface dealing with the general characteristics of the dishes to be described, followed by particular receipts, and the latter often contain amusing little digressions.

Cranberries are brought from America to be sold in London, the reader learns, though those in Wales and Shropshire have far more flavour; pastry was 'the delight of the ancients and of the sensual inhabitants of Asia'; there are frequent warnings against using food out of season, a thing detested by the true gourmet; under 'Ptarmigan' is found an anecdote of Charles XII of Sweden, while under 'Boar's Head' is not only a description of the dish as served through the ages, but also of 'the immortal canvases of Sneiders, Weenix and Rubens' on which it is often to be seen.

The reader discovers that a Paris restaurateur made an immense fortune from *Casserole de Riz au Pieds de Moutons*, that vulgar though delicious dish, and that epicures from all parts of the city came 'trotting after a dinner of trotters'; that steamboats and tunnels—strange conjunction—have driven the salmon from the Thames; that English quails fed in confinement lose 'much of that beautiful flavour they possess in France where they feed in their native vineyards'—and hundreds of other scraps of knowledge from the author's endless store.

As a kind of garnish there are many plates, which were added to in each successive edition. First comes the author's portrait, by his wife, followed by a 'symbolic design'—though it is impossible to guess of what it is the symbol. There is a picture of his 'Table at Home', with the motto 'Une réunion gastronomique sans dames est un parterre sans fleurs, l'Océan sans flots, une flotte maritime sans voiles.' The 'Table of the Wealthy', at which footmen and a page are offering Soyer's pagodatique entrée dish,[1] is inscribed 'Rien ne dispose mieux l'esprit humain à des transactions amicales qu'un dîner bien conçu et artistement préparé.'

[1] See p. 63.

An essay on carving is illustrated with diagrams, including a rather gruesome picture of a half-dissected fowl, and there is a sketch of his newly invented 'tendon separator',[1] and plates, too, of many of his elaborate removes, his patent jelly moulds and attelettes, and a large engraving of the 'Bouquet de Gibier'[2] which he sent to Louis Philippe. A portrait of his wife is followed by a brief account of her life, and some editions also contain an engraving of one of her pictures.

No previous cookery book had supplied plans of labour-saving kitchens of various sizes and for various incomes, and Soyer's series of plans for 'the Kitchen of the Wealthy', 'the Bachelor Kitchen', 'the Cottage Kitchen' and 'my Kitchen at Home' were among the most interesting 'extras'. There is a reproduction of the famous plate of the club kitchens, with a plan, descriptions, and drawings of various details. For each type of kitchen there is a list of the necessary utensils, ranging from the imposing *batterie de cuisine* of the Reform Club, with its eighty stewpans and six meat-saws, to the simple necessities of the cottage kitchen, where 'six black saucepans' take the place of the stock-pots, turbot-kettles, fish-kettles and braising-pans demanded by more luxurious households.

To each edition something new was added, a reprint of the receipt for the *Cream of Great Britain*, his housekeeper's economical way of making coffee, or a 'Monster Bill of Fare found in the Tower of London'. Among these titbits was a *Dialogue Culinaire*, between Lord M. H. (presumably Lord Marcus Hill) and A. Soyer, supposed to take place at the club on 14th May 1846, which sum's up Soyer's views on cooking and eating.[3] 'It occupies no more than two pages,' wrote a reviewer, 'but as Gibbon has said of Tacitus, "they are the pages of Soyer".'

Soyer knew that he was an authority, and no false modesty restrained him from saying so. 'I am entirely satisfied with the composition, distribution and arrangement of my book',

[1] See p. 65.   [2] See p. 66.   [3] See Appendix A.

he wrote, and every critic seemed to agree with him. His confidence, as one of them says, 'is not the arrogant presumption of vanity, but the calm self-reliance of genius.' Flattering reviews appeared in papers so diverse as *John Bull* and the *Petit Courrier des Dames*, *Bell's Life* and the *Court Journal*; *The Times* devoted over three thousand words to an essay on the book, and *Blackwood's Magazine* used it as the text for a long article on 'Cookery and Civilisation'.

Many reviews had political overtones. One Tory confessed that 'with M. Soyer as caterer...we could dine in all love and amity with a Radical or a Repealer, and get "jolly" with a Chartist or an Owenite'; a Reformer hailed the *chef* as 'one of the greatest politicians and pacificators in the world'.

All seemed to agree with the reviewer who thought Soyer 'a wit and a wag of the first water', and so most of the reviews were only half-serious. But even the writer in *Blackwood's*, after pages of laughing with—and at—the author, becomes serious for long enough to insist that the work is 'strictly and most intelligibly practical', and 'as full of matter as an egg is full of meat.' The *Morning Post*, deploring 'certain vulgar errors to which the English adhere with all the consistency of martyrs', is sure that Soyer will rescue them from the most serious of these errors—their treatment of food. And so on endlessly in one paper after another, while the book sold at a prodigious rate, and *The Times* thought it important enough to be given another long review on the appearance of the third edition.

The fascinating description of Soyer's 'Kitchen at Home' awakened great curiosity. Soyer had meant to have this kitchen built in the rooms he shared with Simonau in Leicester Square, but somehow never bothered to see to it—it was not actually constructed until 1849. One lady, an Irishwoman of great determination, made up her mind to see this ideal kitchen, and as a first step decided to commission Simonau to paint her portrait, and then to find out from him the *chef*'s private address.

She went up to Simonau's rooms to make an appointment, expecting to find a large studio or gallery. Instead she found herself in an enormous room, heaped with antiques, old furniture, china, bronzes, draperies and statues, with paintings and drawings everywhere; an unmade bed was in one corner, and in another a feather bed and mattress lay on the floor. On a beautiful table carrots, onions, leeks and a cabbage were heaped in confusion, and an untidy little servant girl, very much down at heel, was preparing some scrag of mutton. The intruder hastily apologised, and explained that she had made an early visit as she lived out of town. Simonau agreed to paint her, and a date for the first sitting was arranged. She was unwilling to leave without Soyer's address, and tried to find excuses for staying.

'Are all these paintings yours?' she asked.

'Many of them are by my pupil, the late Madame Soyer.'

She seized the opportunity. 'But why does M. Soyer leave them here? They would ornament his private house so beautifully.'

'But, madame,' cried Simonau, 'he lives here with me!'

'What!' she was thunderstruck.

'Oh, yes,' said Simonau, 'he lives here. But please excuse me, I must attend to a little culinary business.' He picked up the mutton, and strode through a door, followed by the servant with the vegetables.

'Now or never', thought the visitor, and walked after them. Where was the 'Kitchen at Home'? Where the oven, the *bain-marie*, the hot plate, the 'thick table with sliding shelves and rows of drawers', the 'place for a wet sponge to wipe the table', the 'seasoning-box and fish-sauce box made to turn on centre pivots', the 'dresser with cupboards beneath to put four entrée services of china', the hot water tub, the cold water tub, the draining-board, the plate rack and all the other glories so lovingly and minutely described? She was in a little dark room, where the servant slept, where all the washing and cooking was done, and where everything was in the greatest confusion.

Simonau was surprised to see her appear behind the girl, but was quite unabashed. 'You see, madame, we are very domesticated. We do everything at home. We foreigners must have our own good soups and nourishing stews.'

The visitor had somewhat recovered. 'Do you mean that M. Soyer is going to dine with you?'

'Indeed, madame, he does not make it a rule, but I can assure you he enjoys what I cook, particularly my *potage*.'

'Do you expect him?'

'No, but he may pop in, for we expect the admirable Mlle Cerito for her last sitting, and he will probably come.'

Soyer came in as he spoke, and was struck by the good looks of the lady, who was now blushing deeply. He apologised for interrupting them; 'I do not know', he went on, 'what your business is with my good Simonau, but he is as great an artist in making soup as in painting a picture, and you are therefore in good hands.'

She explained her wish to see the famed 'Kitchen at Home', and Soyer at once replied, 'It would afford me great pleasure, madame, to satisfy your curiosity, but my kitchen at home is out of town, and as I am unfortunately a bachelor....'

Simonau at once took his cue—'Sacresti, madame, I forgot to tell you we have a country box!'

The lady never saw the 'Kitchen at Home', but she had her portrait painted, and was a constant subscriber to Soyer's works. She became an embarrassingly frequent visitor to the club kitchens, so Soyer composed at last some verses 'À la Belle Irlandaise', the first and the last being typical:

> Quand je t'ai vue, adorable Thalie,
>   On aurait dit la Reine de Paphos;
> Tu m'éblouis et ta gorge embellie
>   Eut faire pleurer un marbre de Paros;
> Aussi mon cœur tresaillant d'allégresse,
>   En ta présence a senti de l'émoi;
> Tu révelait le port d'une déesse;
>   Vierge aux yeux noirs, j'ai soupiré pour toi....

La Belle Irlandaise

Si d'un amant tu savais les supplices
   Tu te rendrais à l'ardeur d'Almansor!
Viens avec moi tu sera mes délices,
   Ma déité, mon miroir, mon trésor,
Que ce serment sur ma tête retombe
   Par tous les dieux je te promets ma foi,
Oui désormais jusqu'aux bords de la tombe,
   Vierge aux yeux noirs je n'aimerai que toi.

The results of this declaration are unknown, but the lady's visits to the club abruptly stopped.

CHAPTER V

INVENTIONS

'Sir Politick Would-Be: Sir, I have an ingine...
Peregrine: And call you this an ingine?
Sir Politick Would-Be: Mine own Device....'

BEN JONSON, Volpone

'SOYER' became such a household word that anyone who invented a kitchen appliance tried to persuade the *chef* to attach his name to it. He almost invariably refused. Few men, his vanity insisted, could invent anything which would not diminish his own reputation, and as he could not find time to market his own productions he had none to waste on those of less gifted rivals. Quite apart from the new combinations of food which he created, and the various moulds and attelettes which most *chefs* design for themselves, he was for ever producing some new gadget. This would be proudly displayed to all his visitors for a day or two, then some other notion would occur to him and another invention take the place of honour.

Though naturally most of these things were connected with the preparation or serving of food, Soyer did not confine his passion for improvement to the kitchen. True, he produced new kinds of stoves, varying from his miniature stove for cooking on a table to the great ranges of the Reform Club and to soup-kitchens for feeding thousands daily; he produced all kinds of improved kitchen utensils and machines; he produced bottled relishes, sauces, mustards and punches. But he also invented pantomime transformation scenes, a device for rescuing drowning skaters, a suit which changed its appearance when he pulled a string and a hundred other fantastical curiosities. He was passionately interested in interior decoration, and his transformation of Lady Blessington's elegant

Gore House into his bizarre Symposium of All Nations[1] was a miracle of misapplied ingenuity—and a monument of appallingly bad taste.

Many of his inventions sold well, but he himself never made much money by them, for, like Cézanne, as soon as a creation was perfected he lost interest in it. Soyer would sell the rights of manufacture to any competent person for a few pounds, only insisting that his own name be attached to the finished article. His anxiety to get publicity for his inventions led to his being disparaged as a charlatan. 'That there may have been a slight spice of the *poseur* in his composition it would be idle to deny,' wrote his friend George Augustus Sala, 'but his foible in this direction was a perfectly harmless one, and it was more than compensated by the real talent of the man, by his great capacity for organisation, and by the manliness, simplicity and uprightness of his character.'

In 1848 his first sauces appeared—'one expressly for ladies and the other for gentlemen'[2]—price half a crown. The demand for them was so great that he could not himself prepare the immense quantities required, and he sold the receipts to Messrs Crosse and Blackwell; he was very friendly with the founders of the firm, the first Mr Crosse and the first Mr Blackwell. The bottle, adorned with the inventor's portrait, was of a fantastic bulging shape, and the *Sun* pronounced it 'a most elegant specimen of art manufacture'.

Soyer sent review bottles to all the newspapers, and for once *John Bull* lay down with the *Morning Post*, for once the *Morning Advertiser*, the *Weekly Chronicle*, *Bell's Life*, the *Morning Chronicle* and the *Morning Herald* were unanimous;

[1] See Chapter x.
[2] He often gave two versions of his receipts—one for each sex. The *chef* concocting *Salade de Grouse à la Soyer* or *Salade à la Française*, for instance, was advised to use less eschalot and garlic respectively if ladies were to be of the party; Soyer's *Gelée au Rhum* would, he thought, be 'better appreciated by a party of gentlemen, and should not be introduced where there are ladies'.

the sauce had a magnificent press. *Punch* used the words 'Soyer's New Sauce for Ladies and Gentlemen' as text for a string of jokes—'You all know Soyer the Philanthropist who pretends to be so full of his fellow-creatures?...Was there ever such a cannibal?...No lady, no gentleman is safe. The aristocracy is on the verge of the sauce-boat', and so on.

This first success was followed up by the production of Soyer's Relish, by far the most famous of his sauces, which sold for seventy years. On it, when first invented, the journalists who were given samples exhausted their stock of superlatives. The *Observer* went so far as to declare that the ill-cooked chops which lost Napoleon the battle of Leipsic would have produced a very different effect had they been served up with the Relish.

SOYER'S SAUCE,
Sold only in the above bottles, holding half-a-pint.
Price 2s. 6d.

It became so well known that during a transformation scene in one pantomime, a pumpkin was changed, amid resounding applause, into a bottle of Soyer's Relish.

Soyer also created a concentrated extract of meat, 'Ozmazone', which gained an honourable mention at the Great Exhibition of 1851, a Diamond Sauce, an Aromatic Mustard, and (after his visit to the East) an 'oriental' Sultana's Sauce, with the neck of the bottle appropriately veiled. But apart from the Relish his best known concoction was Soyer's Nectar. In 1848 he had been asked to increase the sales of a new cooling drink, called Tortoni's Anana, by allowing it to bear his name. Not thinking much of the drink as it was, he invented the Nectar to replace it.

Sample bottles were again widely distributed, and again there was an outburst of applause, reminiscent of the modern testimonials for patent medicine. From the Duke of Cambridge to Count d'Orsay, from the *Globe* to the *Lancet*, each new writer was more flattering than the last. 'Imagine,' exclaimed the *Sun*, 'the juices of the most delicious fruits mingled with the scientific dash of a master-hand—the saccharine tartness of the raspberry, the mellow flavour of the apple, a suspicion of quince, an idea of lemon—and all creaming up in a state of effervescence. That is *Soyer's Nectar*!' and the writer warned the inventor to beware lest Jove snatch him up to replace Ganymede.

This marvellous beverage did well for over ten years, though in 1850 Soyer himself had sold his share in it for eight hundred pounds. Private appreciations poured in—many in verse, such as the doggerel:

> When I arise in feverish pain,
> And feel a giddiness of brain,
> What brings back my health again?
> > Soyer's Nectar.
>
> Walking in the cool parterre,
> Fête champêtre or fancy fair,
> What regales the debonair?
> > Soyer's Nectar.

When it is realised that this Nectar was mixed not only with water and soda-water, but also with wine, brandy, maraschino and other liqueurs, it becomes obvious that Soyer, even before the famous Mr Jeremiah Thomas,[1] was the originator of the cocktail.

His innumerable inventions for the kitchen—his Baking-Stewing Pan, his Cooking Clock, his Improved Baking Dish, his Magic Coffee Pot, his patent Egg-Cooking Machine, his Vegetable Drainer, his Chimney Screw-Jack and dozens more —poured out in a seemingly endless stream. On a larger

---

[1] Mr Jeremiah Thomas, inventor of the Blue Blazer, published in 1862 *How to Mix Drinks, or the Bon Vivant's Companion*, which contained receipts for 306 different drinks. It was reissued a few years ago, as the standard authority on the subject.

scale were his Gas Stove—a great novelty—his Detached
Kitchen Range, and his Cottagers' Stove, the latter capable of
'baking, boiling, roasting, washing, ironing, drying linen
and warming rooms of any size'. Most important of all was
the stove he invented for the army, which will be discussed
later.[1] He designed a special 'miniature marine kitchen' to
order, for the steamboat *Guadalquiver*; in a space seventeen
feet by eight he arranged everything necessary for feeding a

The Marquis of N— cooking on a Pyramid with Soyer's Magic Stove

hundred people, and included yet another innovation, 'a
movable balance grating which prevented pans spilling no
matter how the vessel rolled'.

Above all he was proud of his 'Magic Stove', a tiny spirit
stove which he hoped would be useful 'in the parlour of the
wealthy, the office of the merchant, the studio of the artist, or
the attic of the humble'. The press gave it most generous
praise. The *Morning Post* found it 'so certain and cleanly in

[1] See Chapters XIII, XIV, XV.

its operations that a gentleman may cook his steak on the study table, or a lady may have it among her crochet or other work'. The *Morning Chronicle* thought it equally useful for 'the sick room of the invalid, the sportsman on the moors, or the angler by the side of the mountain stream', and had tested it, with gratifying success, in a railway carriage, while the *Morning Advertiser* suggested that the stove could conveniently be carried in its owner's hat.

The Marquis of N— cooking on a Pyramid with Soyer's Magic Stove

The *Sun* welcomed it on behalf of 'soldiers, sailors and sportsmen', and because it would 'emancipate the bachelor living in chambers from the thraldom of his laundress'; the *Globe* recommended it to 'emigrants and tourists' and the *Observer* added to these the name of the epicure, and declared the stove would be an ornament to the table. The Admiralty ordered some stoves for Captain Austin's expedition to the Arctic in search of Sir John Franklin. No. 5 Charing Cross

Road, where the stove was exhibited, was crowded from morning till night, especially when Soyer himself was cooking on it. He was particularly admired for his *rognons de moutons aux fines herbes*, cooked on a drawing-room table, and served to the onlookers with claret, champagne and the Nectar. It became the rage to get Soyer to attend balls with this magic stove, and to cook various dishes for supper in the ball-room itself; *The Times* noted that his *œufs au miroir*, 'half a dozen done every two minutes with the greatest ease and expedition', were a great attraction at a grand ball at Castle Howard, at which the Queen was present.

A noble marquis cooked a meal with the Magic Stove on top of one of the pyramids, and Lieutenant Gale, the balloonist, begged for a stove to take up in his balloon. But there were limits to Soyer's desire for publicity, and realising the danger of fire in the balloon, he wisely refused to give Gale a stove. The balloonist was killed some three weeks afterwards. Soyer had once promised to supply food for a picnic, but when the food was unpacked in the middle of a field, miles from anywhere, the party discovered with horror that it was all uncooked. Soyer, says his secretary, 'called the "spirits" of his stove (and consequently those of his picnic party) from the "vasty deep", and they did "come when he did call them".' The meal was a great success.

The stove was sold alone for thirty-five shillings, or as part of Soyer's 'Magic Kitchen, Expressly adapted for the Overland Route'. Into a box 14 inches by 9 inches by 9 inches was packed everything required to cook and serve a complete meal, including a spice-box, tea-kettle and coffee-pot. There were Magic Kitchens in even smaller sizes, and the Pocket Kitchen was the subject of a dispute between Soyer's friend, Mr George Warriner, and a *douanier*. The latter declared that hardware could not be taken into France. Mr Warriner insisted that the tiny box was his kitchen, and as the officials did not believe him, he produced from a parcel some raw cutlets, already egged and breadcrumbed, threw them into a small pan, lit the stove and served them up in a moment. The kitchen was allowed to pass in.

Sales were so rapid that orders could not be executed; when Soyer toured the provinces exhibiting this stove, in fifteen months over five thousand pounds' worth were sold—but as usual the profit did not go into Soyer's own pockets. He valued more than money the fame implied in the verse by Mr Lee Stevens:

> Soyer, no more to one small class confined,
> With magic stove now cooks for all mankind.
> Pall Mall but just sufficed for his rehearsal,
> The world his Club, his guests are universal.

When by means of all these patent devices the food was cooked, it could be served also with refinements by the same

Pagodatique Entrée Dish

hand. Soyer had a set of entrée dishes made for the Reform Club, with double bottoms containing silver sand which, heated beforehand, remained hot while the entrées were being served. The same principle was employed in his Pagodatique Entrée Dish, which was inspired by the fashionable Chinoiserie, Chinese lacquer, Chinese Quadrilles, 'Exhibitions furiously Chinese'. Soyer remembered that with each entrée the Chinese serve several little dishes containing different sauces, so that each diner can mix his condiments to his own taste. 'Drawn,' he says, 'by the frivolous fancy of fashion and folly of the times; why, I thought, should I not endeavour to make myself as ridiculous as any other person?' He designed a dish with a central circular division, on which the entrée could be served *au naturel*, while various sauces, condiments and pickles could be put into the smaller surrounding compartments. The whole thing was covered with a soaring pagoda-like lid, executed in bright china. Yet another innovation was a *saucière* with a flame below, for serving really hot gravy with venison.

These were all luxurious etceteras; his greatest boon to the ordinary man was his Tendon Separator, for use when carving. Carving was still, as it had been since pupils in ancient Rome practiced on wooden models, a necessary accomplishment. Chaucer's Squire 'carf biforn his fader at the table', and was no doubt well versed in the language and usage of the craft. In the seventeenth century it was 'The Ladies' Delight' to 'barb a lobster, chine a salmon, tranch a sturgeon or culpon a trout', though a hundred years later diners had become more careless. 'I am sure', wrote Dr William King, '*Poets* as well as *Cooks* are for having all Words nicely chosen . . . and therefore I believe they would shew the same Regret that I do, to hear Persons of some Rank and Quality say, *Pray cut up that Goose*; *Help me to some of that Chicken, Hen or Capon, or half that Plover*, not considering how indiscreetly they talk, before *Men of Art*, whose proper terms are, *Break that Goose, Frust that Chicken, Spoil that Hen, Sauce that Capon, Mince that Plover*; if they are so much out in common things, how much more will they be with *Bitterns, Herons, Cranes and Peacocks*?'

Addison had recorded with indignation an instance of a joint being carved at a side-table; Lord Chesterfield held it essential in a well-bred young man 'to do the honours of the table gracefully', since carving badly made a man 'troublesome to himself and disagreeable and ridiculous to others', while Dr Trusler in 1788 wrote: 'We are always in pain for a man who, instead of cutting up a fowl genteely, is hacking for half an hour across a bone, greasing himself and bespattering the company with the sauce.' Not every unskilled carver had the aplomb of the man who knocked the bird he was carving into his neighbour's lap, but finished the story he was telling before turning to her and saying calmly, 'Madame, I'll thank you for that turkey.'

When Peacock's gourmands were lamenting the decay of the art, 'What can be more pitiable', asked the Rev. Dr Opimian, 'than the right-hand man of the lady of the house, awkward enough in himself, with the dish twisted round to him in the most awkward position, digging in unutterable mortification for a joint which he cannot find?' And diners were critical, as witness the royal duke who looked at his plate and exclaimed, 'Take this away, it's a very bad help!'

Soyer hoped to abolish all these agonies and embarrassments. His Tendon Separators resembled the modern sécateurs used in the rose garden, and could be used in the kitchen to disjoint birds before cooking, or on the table itself, if anyone was willing thus to expose his lack of skill.

Not all his inventions were as practical. Six *chefs*—among them two of the Royal Household, the Baroness Rothschild's artiste and Soyer—were competing at Slough for a prize offered for the newest, lightest and most delicate dish. Five creations were placed on the table, four of which were highly praised by the judges, who called for the sixth.

The host carried in a high dish and announced, '*La Croustade Sylphe en surprise à la Cerito*'; the chairman removed the lid, and out darted a beautiful pigeon, which at once flew out on to the terrace and off to London. When the false bottom of the dish was removed, a *salade de filets de grouse à la Bohémienne* was disclosed, and beneath that in yet another compartment some artificial *côtelettes* and mushrooms were resting on a *crème aux pêches*. Soyer had wagered a group of friends that he would send part of a dish from Slough to London quicker than anything except the electric telegraph; the friends were told by telegram when the dish was placed on the table, and fourteen minutes after the telegram had arrived the pigeon flew in, with a paper under its wing on which was written, 'Please pay the *chef de cuisine* of the Reform Club the sum of fifty pounds, for my private apartment in his new dish.'

Soyer's embellishment for a roast peacock must be described by himself. 'In large families where these volatile demi-gods' (so he refers to the peacocks) 'are plentiful, I would recommend them to have one of the finest peacock's tails mounted in silver, and made to easily fix upon the dish, by means of a slide, in which the fowl is served; it would look splendid upon table and remind us of the ancient Roman banquets where' (as the writer insists) 'Lucullus, Tiberius and Horace used to feast and sing their loves.'

In 1846 Louis Philippe was sent a Christmas greeting from England the contents of which, *Punch* remarked, he 'laid nearer to his heart than any missive ever yet written by Aberdeen or Palmerston'. Soyer had created for him a magnificent 'Bouquet de Gibier', a nosegay of game, which was so much appreciated that the king sent in return a pin bearing a bouquet of diamonds and pearls. Soyer's 'Bouquet' was about ten feet high, and proportionately broad. The frame was covered with holly, laurel, mistletoe, evergreens, immortelles, wheat and oats; on this background were arranged twenty-two head of game—larks, snipes, woodcocks, teal, grouse, pheasants, a hare, a leveret and many more; the whole erection was decorated with tricolour ribbons and flags. Louis Philippe summoned the royal family to admire it, had it carried into a Council of Ministers, and—according to *The*

Times—gave orders that it should be copied in wood as a permanent ornament for his dining-room.

Soyer sent another 'Bouquet' to Lord Melbourne, and a third to a lady, with the inscription:

> Madam: Flora having forsaken her flowers,
> I quickly embraced the sport of swift Diana,
> To dedicate and present this bouquet to Venus.

Count d'Orsay—the *arbiter elegantiarum* of the day—insisted that Landseer should be shown so artistic a creation, and for a week or two baskets of fruit or flowers were at a discount; 'Bouquets de Gibier'—for those who could afford them—were all the rage.

'What does it matter where my body happens to be?' the White Knight once remarked. 'The more head downwards I am the more I keep inventing new things.' Soyer had the same imperturbable and ingenious temperament; when saved from drowning by the Royal Humane Society's iceman (after falling through the ice in St James's Park), he not only sent the society a subscription of ten guineas, but also a sketch of an invention for extricating immersed skaters. The society thanked him heartily for both, and at a dinner at the 'Freemasons' Tavern' soon afterwards Soyer led a parade of rescued persons, and returned thanks on their behalf.

CHAPTER VI

BANQUETS

'What an *Hodg-potch* do most that have abilities make in their Stomachs, which must wonderfully oppress and distract Nature: For if you should take *Flesh* of various sorts, *Fish* of as many, *Cabbages, Parsnops, Potatoes, Mustard, Butter, Cheese*, a *Pudden* that contains more than ten several Ingredients, *Tarts, Sweet-meats, Custards*, and add to these *Churries, Plums, Currans, Apples, Capers, Olives, Anchovies, Mangoes, Caveare*, &c., and jumble them altogether into one *Mass*, what Eye would not loathe, what Stomach not abhor such a *Gallemaufrey*? yet this is done every Day, and counted a *Gallent Entertainment*.'

PHYLOTHEUS PHYSIOLOGUS, *Monthly Observations for the Preserving of Health*, 1686

WHEN, after a military expedition into Greece, Paulus Aemilius feasted the Roman people, he found that 'there was equal skill required to bring an Army into the Field and to set forth a magnificent Entertainment; since the one was as far as possibly to Annoy your Enemy, and the other to Pleasure your Friend'. So said Dr William King, and Soyer's friend Pierce carried the comparison a stage further: the *chef* was advised to emulate 'the warrior general who looks forward to the successful termination of his coming engagement', who 'first, with careful study and practised thought, views in prescience each possible exigency, and provides a means to meet it, strategically considering the country in which his scene of action is laid, and the appliances in all respects necessary to his victory'.

This sounds pompous and highfalutin, but the tremendous banquets which Soyer had often to prepare required hours and days and even weeks of careful planning and preparation. Such was the great dinner given to Palmerston, and even more famous was the feast given to Ibrahim Pasha (that Egyptian soldier whom irreverent Cockneys dubbed Abraham

Parker) at the club on 3rd July 1846. The menu of this orgy
is printed in Appendix B, to give some idea of the amount of
organisation needed to produce it successfully.

At the last moment, when Soyer was already dressed to attend
on the Pasha, a message reached him telling of insubordination
among the under-cooks, and he had to strip off his finery, pull
on his red cap, and descend to the kitchens himself to supervise
and encourage his battalions, as a commanding officer might
fling himself into a wavering line and lead it to success.

The dinner was a complete triumph for Soyer; next
morning the press reported the menu as extensively as the
speeches. Lord Panmure wrote to a friend, 'The bill of fare
was worthy of the great Soyer'—the highest possible praise.
When the dessert came on, the *Crème d'Egypte à l'Ibrahim
Pasha* was placed before the guest of honour. It was, says the
Morning Post, 'a pyramid about two and a half feet high,
made of light meringue cake, in imitation of solid stones,
surrounded with grapes and other fruits, but representing
only the four angles of the pyramid through sheets of waved
sugar, to show, to the greatest advantage, an elegant cream
à l'ananas, on the top of which was resting a highly-finished
portrait of the illustrious stranger's father, Mehemet Ali,
carefully drawn on a round-shaped satin *carton*, the exact size
of the top of the cream.' Ibrahim Pasha took up the portrait,
and after showing it to his neighbours with comments on the
clever likeness, carefully put it away. Again turning to the
dish, he saw to his astonishment in the cream, apparently
under glass, a portrait of himself in a gilt frame.

Soyer was sent for, and explained in detail how the picture
had been transferred from wafer paper to the jelly, and how the
gilt frame had been made of *eau de vie de Dantzic* and gold
water mixed with the jelly. Compliments echoed round the
long table, as the admiring guests slid the dish from one to
another. All of it could be eaten, but no one cared to be the
first to break the masterpiece, and though the surrounding
fruit was taken the pyramid was left untouched.

The *Globe* roundly declared that the man of the age was 'neither Sir Robert Peel, nor Lord John Russell, nor even Ibrahim Pasha, but Alexis Soyer'. The writer, however, went on to hope that the fate of the second 'set-piece' at the dinner was not symbolical, for it was a *Gâteau Britannique à l'Amiral* which gave way at the first attack of the spoon, and soon became a wreck.

The Times described it eloquently, 'a comely corvette of cake, coppered with chocolate, displaying wafer sails and sugar rigging, tossing upon waves of *gelée à la Bacchante*—her canvas swelling to a favouring breeze—her sides dripping with wine and marmalade—her interior, even to the hatchways, filled with such freight as none but Soyer could provide and perfect gourmets thoroughly appreciate.' The filling was of delicate vanilla ice, piled with strawberries, cherries, grapes and currants; no wonder that Captain Napier, before whom it was placed, did fearful execution on it. 'Thrusting his boarding-pike—his spoon we should say—' *The Times* goes on, 'deep into the hold of the luscious craft, he destroyed in an instant Soyer's labour of a day. Timbers were stove in or out—sails came down by the run—masts went by the board—and all was wreck where a second before all had been symmetry and perfection.'

In addition to the elaborate general menu some special *tour de force* appropriate to the occasion was created for each banquet. '*Le Soufflé Monstre à la Clontarf*', for instance, appeared at a dinner given to O'Connell at the club on 9th March 1844. This truly monstrous dish was twenty-nine inches high, and seventeen wide; it took four and a half hours to bake, and required thirty-six eggs and other ingredients in proportion. The *Sun* described it: 'Fifty very small soufflés were seen clinging round that colossal mountain, and an extraordinary good likeness of the Great Agitator (drawn on rice paper and surrounded by wreaths of shamrock) appeared as it were rising from the crater.'

Of course this sort of culinary elaboration was nothing new

in England. Food modelled into pictures had always been popular, from the gilt gingerbread men sold at fairs, and the more elaborate gingerbread Valentines of Bath, to that 'subtiltie' at Henry V's coronation banquet, 'an image of St Catherine holding a book and disputing with the doctors', and the less decorous 'sugar subtiltie of a woman in childbed' which was considered a capital joke at a wedding-feast.

At the annual banquet of the Calves' Head Club (founded to ridicule Charles I) various symbolical dishes were served; a cod's head represented Charles Stuart the man, calves' heads dressed in different ways represented Charles the king; a pike with little ones in its mouth was an emblem of tyranny; a boar's head with an apple in its mouth symbolised the king preying upon his subjects. In the eighteenth century the practice flourished in private houses; 'Lord Albemarle's confectioner complained', wrote Horace Walpole, 'that after having prepared a middle dish of gods and goddesses eighteen feet high, his lord would not cause the ceiling of his parlour to be demolished to facilitate their entrée.'

Carême was the great master of the art; after his death frivolity became vulgarity, and by the end of the nineteenth century few private cooks attempted *pièces montées*. At the Savoy Hotel in the 'nineties, however, the glacier was famous for his mountains, castles and polar landscapes carved from ice, with 'white bears of vanilla ice on his snowfields, and the Snow Queen in a meringue cloak on the Jungfrau'. A few years before, a Crucifixion in 'freehand sugar piping' gained a gold medal at a cookery exhibition, and even in the twentieth century we hear of 'a transparent and high decorated pink ice-pudding concealing within inmost recesses a fairy light and a musical box playing the "Battle of Prague"'.

What execrable taste—and how much Soyer would have enjoyed the joke! He had a weakness for these absurd dishes, chiefly as an outlet for his ingenuity and craftsmanship. He enjoyed contriving, say, the 'fictitious ducklings' surmounting his *Turkey à la Nelson*, which were, to quote *The Times*,

'manufactured, we are informed but should never have divined,
of the legs of fowls'. He loved to send up for the second course
apparent joints, made in fact of sponge-cake, carved and iced and
hollowed-out and filled
with fruits and ice-cream;
sometimes, too, sur-
rounded with mock vege-
tables, green currants
for peas, *gelée mousseuse*
for turnips, apples for
potatoes. 'These dishes',
he wrote, 'have often
caused the greatest hila-
rity at table; some parties, unacquainted with them, have
ordered their removal, thinking they belonged to the first
course, whilst others have actually carved them before dis-
covering their mistake.'

Turkey à la Nelson

It must be emphasised that Soyer did not regard such dishes
as more than *jeux d'esprit*, and that he never sacrificed the
palate to the eye. Even the most elaborate devices—the
whipped jelly arranged round the breast and sides of a swan,
'diminishing at the sides by degrees, in imitation of the waves
caused by the bird swimming,' or the *pâté d'office* which formed
the claws of a *petit poussin* or a colossal turkey of sponge-cake—
were eatable to the last fragment, if only the diner had the
heart to destroy the work of art they adorned.

Immense banquets, with all the attendant publicity and *réclame*,
were all very well in their way, but in a dinner on such
a scale there was little room for subtlety, and it was obviously impossible for Soyer to dress many of the dishes
with his own hands. He found another kind of satisfaction
in dressing a dinner personally for a few choice gourmets,
whose praises would be informed, and who would not be
taken in by the fine appearance of a dish if the flavour was not
equally perfect.

In May 1846 Soyer served what he described as 'the most recherché dinner I ever dressed' for a party of ten epicures at the Reform Club; the menu is given in Appendix C. The ingredients for the dishes were ordered a week before, mullets and salmon from Grove's, other fish from Jay's, foie gras and truffles from Morel's, saddleback of lamb from Newlands's, Welsh mutton from Slater's, every tradesman furnishing his own speciality. Expense was not considered; the dish of crawfish, when dressed, cost upwards of seven guineas. At seven o'clock the live Severn salmon, newly arrived from Gloucester, was brought to Soyer, and 'was boiled immediately, being just ten minutes before the dinner was placed upon the table, and was eaten in perfection', while the mullets were the finest the *chef* had ever seen.

The diners were more than satisfied, but not so Soyer; he had planned one more dish, and a change in the weather had held up the ortolans ordered for it from Paris. He had already obtained twelve of the finest and largest truffles, in each of which—since one cannot stuff an ortolan with a truffle —he had intended to bury an ortolan. 'This', said a modern gourmet, 'is sometimes called *Ortolan-in-the-Coffin*; such a coffin as one would die for.'

CHAPTER VII

SOUP-KITCHENS: IRELAND
AND SPITALFIELDS

'Beautiful Soup! who cares for fish,
Game or any other dish?
Who would not give all else for two p
ennyworth only of beautiful Soup?'

LEWIS CARROLL, *Alice's Adventures in Wonderland*

'In a disputed will case, one of the witnesses kept saying he knew the
testator was a man of sound mind and that he led a godly and pious life.
The judge asked, "What do you mean by a man leading a godly and
pious life?"—"Please your lordship, he spent most of his time and
money in teaching the poor to make cheap soup."'

Buckmaster's Cookery

WHILE Soyer was enjoying his greatest fame at the club,
regaling the members with some new delicacy every day, the
people of England were passing through the 'Hungry
'Forties'. There were indeed, in Disraeli's words, two nations
in England. The members of the club and their peers sat
down to tables almost literally groaning under a profusion of
dishes and delicacies; the poor lived on tea and bread and
potatoes and cheese, with meat once, or at the most twice, a
week.

In 1845 wet weather ruined the corn harvest in England,
and a blight wiped out the potato crop in Ireland. Bread in
England had been so dear for thirty years that the poor had
not been able to afford much of it, but in Ireland potatoes
were the staple food of the peasants; with no potatoes, with
no corn from England, with the Corn Laws preventing supplies
of corn coming in from abroad, the people of Ireland ate grass
and died in the streets. In 1846 the potato crop, after
promising well, failed again, and in four years the population

of Ireland was reduced from over eight millions to six and a half millions. Nearly a million people starved to death and nearly a million emigrated. The repeal of the Corn Laws in 1846 stopped the rise in the price of bread, but did not reduce it; the condition of the people grew worse and worse.

Soyer had been for some time giving private classes to charitably inclined ladies[1] to teach them, as Florence Nightingale's Aunt Ju told her, to make soup for 'the hungry poors'. Early in 1847 he decided that his methods were worth a wider trial, and he originated a public subscription for soup-kitchens for the poor, heading the list himself with a gift of thirty pounds. Soon one kitchen in Leicester Square was distributing forty to fifty gallons of soup to two or three hundred people daily, and in his usual grandiose manner Soyer sketched out plans for supplying twenty thousand people, and invented a new type of soup-boiler.

The publication of his receipts in *The Times* aroused a storm of pæans and protests, and started a long correspondence in the columns of the paper, while their author received hundreds of personal letters. The day after his first letter appeared, a friend dashed up to him at the club, breathless with haste.

'Dripping's up!' he gasped.

'What?' said Soyer.

'If you'd told me you meant to specify dripping in your receipts,' said his friend, 'I could have gone into the market and bought tons of dripping—we could have cleared some hundreds!'

The *chef* collapsed in roars of laughter, but soon he had to deal with more serious criticism. He had asserted that his soups had been 'tasted by numerous noblemen, members of Parliament and several ladies...who had considered it

---

[1] Perhaps it was one of these ladies who horrified her solicitor by insisting on leaving money to supply the poor with a 'Brothel'—after her death a receipt was found among her papers, headed in an elegant sloping Victorian hand, 'Excellent Broth for the Brothel'.

very good and nourishing', but Mr Jacquet disagreed with these judges. Jacquet was the proprietor of an alamode beef-house, and was perhaps inspired by professional jealousy, though he professed only to be anxious lest 'an article recommended by M. Soyer should be considered by the nobility and public as the standard receipt for soups for charitable purposes, and thereby a serious injury inflicted on the recipients of their bounty'. In short, he thought Soyer's receipts would produce not 'soup for the poor', but 'poor soup'—'an innutritious compound as will only tend to weaken and destroy the constitution'.

Much vexation was expressed by 'No Cook' ('a house-keeper with a family of nine'), who had tried the receipt and found the cost three-halfpence and not—as Soyer had said—three-farthings a quart, and therefore accused him of 'great injury to the poor by misrepresenting the price of necessities'. 'Medicus', from the Athenæum, denied that 'a basinful of M. Soyer's soup once a day, together with a biscuit', could sustain anyone, and dared Soyer and 'the best judges of the noble art of gastronomy at the Reform Club' to try such a diet for a week or two.

Soyer replied with spirit that only the continual demand for soup had delayed his answer to three 'stomachable' letters, and proceeded to deal with his decriers seriatim. Jacquet, who had objected to the small quantity of meat required, was challenged to distinguish with his 'scientific palate' between soups made by Soyer with and entirely without meat; 'in compounding the richest soups', it was explained, 'the balance of it is the great art. I can myself [with a much greater proportion of meat] make a most insipid, detestable and innutritious soup by not preparing it *secundum artem*.' 'No Cook' was offered free instruction to make her one, and her figures disputed, while with regard to living on the soup —'I beg to inform the writer', declared Soyer, 'that for the last three weeks I have made so many soups, and continually tasting of each, that I have actually fed on it (barring the biscuit) and I assure you, sir, that all the nobility and gentry, now daily visiting me, say that I look as well as ever.'

Punch suggested that Soyer 'must have prepared the new Prussian Diet'—the Frankfort Parliament—'for it is so like his soup, there's nothing in it'. Indeed, for quite a time Soyer's soup was *Punch*'s staple jest. Was the soup lacking in meat? Then, said *Punch*, use the game which destroys English crops —'If the Irish eat up the game, the game will not eat up the farmer.... Instead of making game of Soyer's soup, let Soyer's soup be made of game, and the extirpation of game by Soyer's instrumentality will add appropriate lustre to a name associated with Reform.' Or why not add an Irish bull to the soup? The *chef* was 'a broth of a boy', and an Irishman was made to say damningly, 'The soup is delicious—for the more I take of it the more it brings the water into my mouth.'

Meanwhile, the thrower of the stone which started all these ripples had left theory for practice. The sufferings of the English poor were bitter enough, but the state of the Irish was infinitely worse. Existing pauperism became famine, which was followed by pestilence; the wretched people, without adequate clothes or coverings, ill-lodged and starving, died like flies; they perished so quickly that there was a chronic shortage of coffins to bury the dead. Whole parishes were reduced to extremes of destitution, and more than once murder was committed for a handful of flour or a few rotten potatoes. In January 1847 Lord John Russell had announced that the Government proposed to appoint relief committees for the worst districts, to be responsible for purchasing food, erecting soup-kitchens, and distributing meals to the starving Irish. The need can be deduced from the figures: in June 1847 over three million people were being entirely supported by these committees.

The Government, at the request of the Lord Lieutenant of Ireland, invited Soyer to submit to them his much-discussed plan for a new type of soup-kitchen, and suggested that instead of erecting it in London he should first go to Ireland, and superintend the building of a model kitchen in Dublin. The club gave him special leave of absence, and by the middle of March he was supervising the making of soup from his receipts in various Dublin hospitals and workhouses, while the new model kitchen was being built as quickly as possible in a large railed-in space in front of the Royal Barracks.

The model kitchen was opened on 5th April. It was a wooden building about forty by fifty feet, in the centre of which was a steam boiler, with a three-hundred-gallon pan above it and an oven heated by the same fire at one end. Eight iron pans on wheels held various ingredients which were cooked by steam from the boiler. At each end of this apparatus were cutting tables and chopping-blocks, where ingredients were prepared, and round two roof-supports were condiment boxes. Long tables into which a hundred bowls were let in, with a hundred spoons attached by chains, stood at one end of the building; tin water-tanks for the washing of the bowls were behind each table.

Outside, a zig-zag passage—true Soyer touch—led a hundred people at a time to a side-door. A bell was rung, they entered and drank their soup while the passage refilled from the waiting crowd. Having eaten, the people went out through a little room where bread and biscuits were distributed. Carts and barrows with fires beneath took large quantities of soup to other distributing centres. Soyer calculated that five thousand meals a day could be supplied, and in fact from 6th April to 14th August 1,147,279 rations were distributed, an average of 8750 daily.

The poor were supplied from 6th April onwards; on 5th April it had been the turn of the nobility and gentry, who came by invitation to inspect the rather Heath Robinson apparatus. Soup was served to a brilliant gathering, including Prince George of Cambridge and the Lord Chancellor, and even including, perhaps, some of those landlords who were still exporting grain to England while their tenants died at their doors from starvation, or crept to the distributing centres to beg for Government rations.

In a few days the scheme proved so successful in producing better food at a lower cost that the Government bought the kitchen, and handed it over to the South Union Relief Committee of Dublin. In September a balance-sheet was published showing that the kitchen had saved the ratepayers in the South Union some £7768, almost exactly half the usual cost of the food, and that these ratepayers had paid only a shilling in the pound, while their fellows in the North Union where relief was given under the old system had paid three shillings and fourpence.

The *chef* returned to the club with his reputation much enhanced and with a material souvenir in the shape of 'a very elegant snuff-box', presented to him at a dinner in his honour in Dublin. A second public dinner was given at the 'London Tavern', at which more than a hundred and fifty people toasted Soyer. It was a very grand affair altogether; in contrast to the tin basins of the soup-kitchens the service was of gold and silver plate.

Ballads about Soyer's Irish mission were sold in the streets. Typical is an *Ode to Soyer* which declared:

> ...Amidst the din of party strife,
> Illustrious *chef*! you bare the knife
> To save—not to extinguish—life...
> For place or pension many fight,
> *You* only war with *appetite*....

After comparing him with Ude, Mrs Glasse, Miss Acton and Dr Kitchiner, to their great disadvantage, it went on,

> Yet, Soyer, great as was thy fame,
> New glories now adorn thy name;
> For though the rich thy art did claim
> Thou's heard'st the poor man's cry...

and ended with a picture of Emma looking down approvingly from Heaven, while Soyer's name was handed down to future generations of cooks as a true 'Regenerator'.

Many people had written to ask Soyer where copies of his economical receipts could be found, so while in Ireland he published a sixpenny booklet of fifty pages, *Charitable Cookery, or The Poor Man's Regenerator*, all profits from its sale being given to charity. It begins with an 'Address to the World in General, but to Ireland in Particular', containing a description of the 'desolate and harrowing scenes of misery and death' which he was seeing in Ireland. 'But permit me to ask you,' he writes, 'What are the efforts, even of a civilised nation, against the will of the Almighty? With me you will justly answer useless.' He implores everyone 'to use and not abuse Nature's productions', and remarks that 'it requires more science to produce a good dish at trifling expense than a superior one with unlimited means'.

Deploring the usual 'soups' distributed to the poor, he proceeds to give better receipts, and (as usual in advance of his time) begs everyone to use the outside of vegetables, '*using* that which has hitherto only increased the malaria of our courts and alleys by its decomposition'. Receipts are given not only for soup, but for economical puddings and stews, substitutes for bread, and the like.

Aided by flattering press notices, the booklet had a large sale. Its author was getting a reputation for this sort of work and soon after his return to England the Royal Agricultural Society asked him to contribute articles to their journal on provisions for famine, on substitutes for potatoes (the blight was still active) and on making cheap nutritious soup on a large scale. The last receipt was to be used in big country houses, and the soup distributed weekly to the labourers' families. 'A hint from M. Soyer', the letter optimistically declared, 'would no doubt make this soup equal to mock-turtle soup, at a trifling expense.' He was also asked to write a substitute for the Society's *Cottage Tract on Cookery*, and offered them *The Poor Man's Regenerator*.

These philanthropic activities had received a good deal of

publicity, and Soyer was inundated with begging letters. He was generous to the point of ostentation; if an acquaintance produced a subscription list Soyer would say, 'Is it all right, my dear fellow? Put me down for a couple of guineas', and a hard luck story almost always drew a sovereign or two from him. When he heard of distress too universal to be dealt with single-handed, he appealed to others to help him, and a year after his Irish expedition he again wrote to *The Times* to beg for the poor.

A visit to Spitalfields had disclosed scenes of horrible destitution: 'Five or six in a small room, entirely deprived of the common necessities of life', he wrote, 'no food, no fire, and hardly any garment to cover their persons, and that during the late severe frost; the only piece of furniture was the weaving machine, now silent.' With the aid of the vicar Soyer had himself established a soup-kitchen which fed three hundred and fifty children daily, but there were ten thousand poor people in the parish, and very few wealthy parishioners who could be asked to help. Soyer appealed for funds to continue and extend the work until every stricken parish had its own kitchen, supplying daily to every hungry man, woman and child a quart of soup and some bread for a penny.

The subscription made slow progress; in that year starvation was universal, and every private purse had endless calls made upon it. In May Soyer thought of a new way to raise funds. He held an exhibition of Emma's drawings and paintings—a hundred and forty of them—calling it 'Soyer's Philanthropic Gallery'. The invitation cards for the private view were cut into rhomboids and fancifully painted; on the opening day the staircase was decorated with flowers and the *chef* received the visitors.

The Times applauded his taste: 'There is a sort of comfortable sensation in the saloon', wrote a reporter, 'as if the walls were peopled by lively good-humoured personages.' He liked the catalogue, too, with its portrait of Madame Soyer and its 'fund of pleasant anecdotes', and thought it 'an amusing book *per se'*. Despite all these attractions only two hundred and sixty pounds were collected; this supplied over fifty thousand rations in Spitalfields, but the bigger scheme had to be shelved.

The kitchen which had been started in Leicester Square in 1847 had soon been closed from lack of funds, but it was opened again early in 1848, Soyer devoting much of his time to planning and supervision. Prince Albert was graciously pleased to visit it and taste the soup, subscriptions grew more plentiful, and for the next five years soup and bread were constantly supplied to the poor. Soyer was always ready to help with advice, to dun his wealthy acquaintances for subscriptions, and to suggest improvements in the receipts and apparatus.

CHAPTER VIII

'THE MODERN HOUSEWIFE'

'To speak then of the knowledges which belong unto our British House-wife—I hold the most principal to be a perfect skill in COOKERY: Shee that is utterly ignorant therein, may not by the Lawes of strict Justice challenge the freedom of Marriage; because indeede Shee can perform but half her vow, Shee may love and obey but Shee cannot cherish and keepe her Husband.'

GERVASE MARKHAM, *English Housewife*, 1637

SOYER had now 'regenerated' the kitchens of the very poor and the very rich, but had neglected the middle class—the class which was then so rapidly growing in size and importance. True, the *Morning Advertiser* had advised 'every housewife who wishes to enjoy comfort herself and be the cause of it in others' to study earnestly the section of the *Gastronomic Regenerator* devoted to the 'Kitchen at Home', but the book was very expensive and was designed for the *chef* or *cordon bleu* rather than the ordinary cook. So Soyer began to prepare a work on a simpler plan, which he called *The Modern Housewife or Ménagère*.

It is dedicated to a friend of his, a Mrs Baker, of Bifrons Villa, St John's Wood, whom he regarded as a model house-keeper, and she is the 'Hortense' who is nominally the author of the book. In the preface is found a conversation between Mr and Mrs B. and their departing guest Mrs L., who has been so impressed by Mrs B.'s ménage that she begs her to reveal some of her secrets. Mr B. speaks: '"Certainly, my dear madam; in my wife, without flattering her too much, you see almost an accomplished woman" (in hearing such praise Mrs B. retired, saying "How foolishly you talk, Richard") "she speaks two or three different languages tolerably well, and as an amateur is rather proficient in music, but her parents, wisely considering household knowledge to be of the greatest importance, made her first acquainted with the keys of the storeroom before those of the piano; that is the only secret, dear madam".' The book consists of letters between Mrs L. (Eloise) and Mrs B., the latter instructing her friend in every department of housewifery, cooking of all kinds, the nursery dinner,[1] comforts for invalids, the management of servants, guests and children.

The letters which accompany each batch of receipts give a complete picture of the rise of a middle-class Englishman of the time, from a beginning as a small shopkeeper to prosperity as a well-to-do merchant. The B.'s had begun married life quite humbly. 'When we first commenced housekeeping', writes Mrs B., 'we were six in family, five of whom breakfasted together, the three young men in the shop, Mr B. and myself'; the sixth was the servant girl. She shows how she fed this household plainly but well on thirty-two shillings a week. Sunday's dinner was 'Roast Beef, potatoes, greens and Yorkshire Pudding; Monday's, Hashed Beef and potatoes; Tuesday's Broiled Beef and Bones, Vegetables and Spotted Dick Pudding'; they had as well 'a Good Breakfast and Tea' and when from time to time a friend joined them at dinner some little extra dish was added to the usual menu.

Later their income increased a little (but the three young men still dined with them) and the dinners became more elaborate. On Sunday, the dinner was 'Pot-au-Feu, Fish, Haunch of Mutton or a Quarter of Lamb or other good Joint, two vegetables, pastry and fruit puddings, a little Dessert' and meals on the same scale were served throughout the week. Their parties, too, became larger (though there were never more than ten people present) and they had perhaps 'Julienne Soup, Fish, a Quarter of Lamb, Vegetables and Cutlets,

[1] Sir Erasmus Wilson, a medical authority, said that this was one of the most valuable pages that he ever read on the subject of diet, and was 'calculated to confer an everlasting benefit on society'.

Vegetables and Bacon and Beans, Boiled Turkey, Pheasant, Jelly or Cream, Pastry, Lobster Salad, Omlet or Soufflé, Dessert, Etc.'

Finally, Mr B. became very well-off indeed. Mr and Mrs B. dined alone, or with a friend, and their daily bill of fare was 'one soup or fish (generally alternate)—one remove, either joint or poultry—one entrée—two vegetables—pudding or tart—a little dessert'. 'This', Mrs B. explains, 'may seem a great deal for two persons; but when you remember that we almost invariably have one or two to dine with us, and the remains are required for the breakfast, lunch, nursery and servants' dinners, you will perceive that the dinner is the principal expense of the establishment, by which means you are enabled to display more liberality to your guests, and live in greater comfort without waste.'

In *The Modern Housewife* the social historian can find details of the various entertainments which the B.'s gave, and it is pleasant to notice how as years passed Mr B.'s birthday party grew grander and grander, until the dessert alone consisted of nineteen dishes. Children's parties are also described; Mrs B. sadly notes that though her children now have fifty guests at a time and supply an elaborate meal, they are no happier than they were in the days when the refreshments were merely 'sandwiches and patties and plain sweets', when 'we used to amuse the children by labelling the dishes as "Sandwiches of Peacock's Tongues", "Patties of Partridges' Eyes"'—the pen is held by Mrs B., but the voice is the voice of Soyer.

To show the difference between even the grandest menus served by Mrs B. and 'high-class cookery' two splendid bills of fare are given. One is of a dinner carried out by Soyer at the Reform Club for an M.P., and the other of a party at the christening of Sir George Chetwynd's grandson in Warwickshire, which Soyer went down to arrange, taking with him as a christening gift for the baby 'the proof copy of his new work on cookery—*The Modern Housewife*'.

The book was published in the autumn of 1849, and within a fortnight a second edition of six thousand copies had to be rushed through the press. It sold in quantity for many years (the twenty-first thousand was published in 1851 and the thirtieth thousand in 1853), and brought the author an even larger income than that supplied by the more expensive *Gastronomic Regenerator*.

The Modern Housewife was rapturously received by the press. Every paper in the kingdom—from the *Edinburgh Courant* to the *Exeter Flying Post*, from the *Bristol Mercury* to the *Norfolk News*—sang its praises.

Publisher, reviewers, readers, everyone was satisfied—except the author. To each new edition he added new plates, new receipts, new anecdotes. In 1853, when the thirtieth thousand appeared, the readers learnt of a revolution in the B.'s fortunes. 'The too bold speculation of your unfortunate but devoted husband', as Eloise put it, had reduced them to poverty, but Mr B., though now only a Head Clerk on the Railway, was luckily 'quite as happy and more settled in mind' than when they were better off.

Hortense writes from 'Camelia Cottage', near Rugby, which she has renamed because she thought 'Rabbit Cottage' a 'very unclassical name'. Though now she has only one servant, and does the cooking herself, she is quite undaunted; 'Knowing how to make much of a little is the first of domestic qualifications; adversity gives birth to genius.' And genius she has, for she manages to buy 'an ox-cheek and palates, an ox foot boiled, two sheep's heads, twelve sheeps' brains, one ox kidney, twelve onions, a few leeks, carrots, turnips, a little thyme, bayleaves, a few cloves, salt and pepper' all for three shillings and threepence.

This edition has many entirely new sections, including the 'Physiology of Tarts', with illustrations, a complete cottage cookery, and a reprint of *The Poor Man's Regenerator* to suit Hortense's new circumstances. But she has not forgotten more prosperous days, and there are some shrewd remarks on fashionable bachelors, and an admirable new description of a dinner-party, with comprehensive advice to the hostess. 'In the dessert I generally introduced some new importation, such as bananas, sugar-cane, American lady-apples, prickly pears, etc. These also give a subject for the gentlemen to talk about when the ladies have left, as free trade, colonial policy, etc.'

Five years after the first appearance of *The Modern Housewife*, a newspaper correspondent who was at Scutari en route for the Crimean expedition wrote that 'the officers, being compelled to cook for themselves, have with the aid of Soyer's *Housewife* and their servants, attained a degree of culinary skill which would astonish their friends at home'. At the same time an American mission staying in Sebastopol with the Russians kept themselves well fed by following the advice of the same book.

CHAPTER IX

RESIGNATION: WORK IN
THE PROVINCES

'With preference mark him, who, proud of his station,
Conceives himself born for the good of the nation;
In the kitchen with dignity lays down the law,
Uncontroul'd, in his sphere, as a Turkish Bashaw.'

BERCHOUX, *Poem on Gastronomy*

THE real reason for Soyer's departure from the Reform Club
is a mystery. Ostensibly, it was a change in the rules about
the admission of visitors to the Coffee Room. Soyer said that
if they were to be admitted every day, instead of twice a week
as the custom was, the club would become a mere restaurant.
He himself—so he declared—did not care what they made of
it, but he would have to increase the kitchen staff, and could
not give the same attention to the cooking. He would therefore retire as soon as the committee could find a cook to suit
them. Three months later the alteration was made; Soyer
resigned, and was succeeded by a M. Guerrir.

He remained on the friendliest terms with most members of
the committee; past unpleasantnesses were forgotten, and
Lord Marcus Hill, the chairman, expressed the great regret
which the committee felt at their *chef*'s resignation. Unanimously, he wrote to Soyer, the committee had desired him to
express 'the high sense which they entertain of your past
services, as well as of the zeal, ability, perfect integrity and
uniform respectability of conduct which you have devoted to
the well-being of the Club during a period of nearly thirteen
years' duration'. Lord Marcus sent also his own wishes for
Soyer's health and happiness, and it was to Lord Marcus
personally that the *chef* replied.

'My Lord,—Il y aurait ingratitude de ma part, si je quittais les rênes du départment culinaire du Reform Club sans remercier le gentilhomme par excellence, qui souvent, par son jugement impartial et les preuves de son amitié constante, fut la cause que je les aie guidés si long-temps.

'Vous, my Lord, qui savez parfaitment ce que c'est que de tenir un établissement particulier, croirez bien qu'après treize années de travaux, d'anxiété et de responsabilité continuel, tel que ma place l'exigeait au club, les années pourraient presque se compter double sur la tête d'un homme qui n'a pas eu à s'occuper de travaux ordinaires, pour preuve j'en atteste à mes cheveux blancs, qui ne comptent pas encore quarante printemps.

'Malgré que je me retire entièrement de la cuisine, j'ai des offres très-avantageux et de haute importance, que j'aimerais beaucoup vous soumettre, pour recevoir de vous les conseils d'un ami, basés sur cette amitié cordiale que vous n'aurez jamais occasion de changer.

'Veuilliez avoir l'extrême obligeance, my Lord, de remercier mille fois les membres du comité pour la charmante lettre que votre âme noble a dictée, et qu'ils ont aussi unanimement et cordialement approuvés.'

The news of Soyer's resignation was received by the members, the press and the public with amazement and incredulity. Soyer was an institution at the club, he had designed its kitchens, he had made its culinary reputation, he had indeed—according to the Tories—been the real reason of its enormous membership. 'The Reform is known to the world at large', wrote the author of a guide-book in 1851, 'as being the club where the inimitable Soyer presided for so long a period.' He was as much a part of the club as the marble bust of the queen in the great saloon and the picture of Lord Holland in the hall. He was earning upwards of a thousand a year, his salary being increased by fees received from apprentices and 'improvers', since a cook trained by Soyer could demand wages of five or six pounds a month, when ordinary cooks received about ten pounds a year.

King Soyer resigning the Great Stewpan (from *Punch*)

Punch pictured the affecting scene—'King Soyer resigning the great stewpan'; already, it was said, the *chef* had received the 'most liberal offers' if he would become director of several railway companies, and help to 'cook their accounts'. Indeed, some of the 'most advantageous and important offers' to which Soyer's letter referred were almost as absurd. It was proposed that he should open new restaurants and eating-houses of every kind, here, there and everywhere, and preside over old ones; that he should found 'a college of domestic economy' and 'a school of cookery'; that he should make a business of supplying city banquets. He was invited to conduct a gastronomic tour of France, and another of Paris.

The last suggestion appealed to him, and he promised to think it over. At once the promoter published a prospectus, offering an elaborate programme. A *déjeuner à la fourchette*, promenade and foot-race in the forest of Fontainebleau, a *fête champêtre* at Rambouillet, a *fête dansante* in the Bois de Boulogne, a *fête musicale* in the Jardin d'Hiver, a *fête Venitienne* at Asnières, a collation at Versailles, a picnic at St Germain—all these delights and many others, under Soyer's leadership, with first-class travel from London to Paris and back, were offered for the remarkably modest sum of fifteen guineas.

The Paris correspondent of the *Globe* picked up some story about the proposed excursion, and Soyer's angry letter to the editor is an excellent example of his style when on his dignity. 'Mr Editor,' he began, 'In reading your Paris correspondent of Monday last, I was not a little surprised to see my name in connection with a *supposed agent*, whose industry led him—my prospectus in hand—to hunt all the hotel-keepers in the fashionable quarter of Paris, to make room for a monster party of six hundred excursionists from London; and that owing to this sort of speculation being at a discount, I had been obliged (notwithstanding my magnificent prospectus) to reduce the anticipated number to one hundred.

'This leaves an impression that I intended to make a monster speculation. Allow me, Mr Editor, to observe that I have not appointed any agent whatsoever in Paris for the object above-mentioned; but merely confined myself to exchanging a few letters with one of the first hotel-keepers there to insure the comfort of my friends; and secondly, that my magnificent prospectus is only intended for a select party of acquaintances whom, at their own request, I have consented to lead and entertain in a manner never hitherto attempted, both as regards the gratification of sight-seeing in the capital of France and its environs, but also to give them a full opportunity of judging what can be done in the way of living when led by a gastronomic caterer.'

It is a nice question whether he was more indignant at the suggestion that he was a speculator or at the insinuation that he speculated unsuccessfully. In any case the false publicity and the taking for granted of his consent enraged him so much that the party never took place.

Everyone who attempted to influence the *chef*'s plans made the same mistake; they presented him with a detailed scheme to which he was expected to conform. They forgot that he prided himself above all on his independence and originality, and he inevitably refused to carry out any plan which he had not himself conceived. During the latter half of 1850 he was kept busy organising banquets all over the country, demonstrating his inventions and revising his books, and refused to come to any decision about his future.

Soyer's friend Mr Lumley, director of Her Majesty's Theatre, gave a *fête champêtre* every summer, to which not only actors, singers and dancers were invited, but also the patrons of the theatre and all Mr Lumley's acquaintances among the nobility. On one occasion Prince Louis Napoleon danced a quadrille in the same set as Lumley, Cerito, Taglioni and Carlotta Grisi, and these parties were always regarded as among the most pleasant of the season. This year Lumley wished to honour Scribe and Halévy, whose adaptation of Shakespeare's *Tempest* he was producing. After consultation with Soyer, he invited a thousand guests to visit him on 19th June.

The refreshments were on the grandest scale; the centre-piece was entitled *Croustade Shakespearienne à la Halévy-Scribe*, and was a model of the ship in the *Tempesta* as it was wrecked by Ariel's magic. 'The addition of two *chartreuses de pêches*', wrote the *Globe*, 'in imitation of barrels, for cargo, were in the interior of the dilapidated vessel; on the top of each was seen, through a very clear jelly, beautifully framed, the portraits of the two celebrated French visitors. The waves were represented by spun sugar and transparent jelly, and the wrecked cargo by grapes, peaches, apricots, etc., floating round the ship.'

The guests were delighted by the creation, which they regarded as a great compliment; Madame Scribe thanked Soyer for the honour done to her husband, and he replied, 'Honour! Madame, no honour could exceed his greatness; for if the shade of Molière were to rise from his tomb, it would be jealous of his talents.'

This was all very pleasing, but there was another interpretation of the dish. *Punch* regarded it as a satire and a criticism: 'The shattered ship in *pain d'Espagne*, with the characters of the *Tempest* in sugar, gaudily coloured, tossed by a sea of trifle and stranded on a reef of bon-bons—illustrating, how happily, the treatment that the illustrious William had received at the hands of Messrs Scribe and Halévy.'

In July 1850 the Royal Agricultural Society asked Soyer to organise their annual dinner, to be held at Exeter. The local tradesmen, annoyed because the contract had gone to a Frenchman who might order all his provisions from London, were prepared to be as disobliging as possible. But as soon as Soyer arrived he engaged the town-crier to announce that all tradesmen willing to supply food were invited to meet the *chef* at his hotel—this changed the feelings of the shopkeepers and was also excellent publicity. It was Soyer's first big public dinner in the provinces, and he was determined to make it a memorable occasion.

The dinner was held in an enormous pavilion, designed for a thousand guests. At one end of the marquee Soyer erected an arch, seventeen feet high and twelve wide, symbolic of triumphant agriculture. A beef-eater stood on either side, and it was decorated with all sorts of animals and vegetables —a swan, a large barn-door cock, geese, turkeys, rabbits, lambs, pigeons, ducks and hens, all whole; the heads of pigs, bullocks and stags; carrots, cucumbers, turnips, cabbages, onions and leeks; sheaves of corn, fruits, flowers and laurels; coloured ribands and flags, a plough, a rake, a hoe, a spade; all these were piled into a magnificent frame, surrounding at first a boar's head, and later Soyer's much-admired novelty— an ox roasted whole by gas.

In the Castle yard a brick oven was built, with an iron cover. The enormous joint, weighing five hundred pounds, was put in, gas pipes were arranged round it and lit, and after four and a half hours a band playing loudly, with colours flying, escorted the monster dish to the pavilion, where it was received with acclamation and declared perfectly cooked.

Twelve hundred people sat down to a gargantuan meal. These farmers, like the Hambledon cricketers, 'could no more have pecked in that style than they could have flown, had the infernal black stream (that type of Acheron!) which soddens the carcass of a Londoner, been the fertiliser of their clay.' This was no place for subtleties and French kickshaws—the menu shows that the *chef* could adapt his art to a country feast. At one end was a *Baron of Beef à la Magna Charta*, at the other the arch. On the tables were ranged:

> Thirty-three dishes of ribs of beef.
> Thirty-five dishes of roast lamb.
> Ninety-nine dishes of galantine of veal.
> Twenty-nine dishes of ham.
> Sixty-six dishes of pressed beef.
> Two rounds of beef *à la Garrick*.

Two hundred and sixty-four dishes of chicken.

Thirty-three French raised pies *à la Soyer*.

One hundred and ninety-eight dishes of spring mayonnaise salad.

Two hundred and sixty-four cherry, gooseberry, raspberry and currant tarts.

Thirty-three Exeter puddings (invented for the occasion).

One hundred and ninety-eight dishes of hot potatoes.

No one kitchen could produce such a supply. Kitchens all over the town were used, and though heavy rain drummed on the roof and drenched the messengers who carried the dishes from kitchens to table, all went well inside the pavilion. Soyer was everywhere at once, admonishing here, encouraging there, clearing up confusion and somehow keeping an eye on every table. The Earl of Chichester declared it the society's most successful dinner, and invited the *chef* to repeat his achievement in succeeding years.

There was a great deal of cooked food left untouched, and Soyer suggested that it should be used to give a dinner to the poor of the city, and that a subscription should be taken up to cover any extra expenses. The well-fed company responded generously, and about seven hundred poor people were feasted the next day.

Soyer became vastly popular in the town, and received many invitations, addressed not so much to the cook as to the lively and sociable man. Before leaving Exeter he wrote to the local press thanking everyone for their kindness, help and hospitality, and promising to send to the editor for insertion in the paper a perfected receipt for the Exeter Pudding invented for the dinner. The editor begged him to send the pudding itself, which would cheerfully be inserted in the proper quarter.

And so Soyer came back to London, leaving great goodwill behind him. He had made no financial profit—indeed he was considerably out of pocket by the time all the accounts were settled—but that seemed of no importance at all when he thought of the glowing reports in the press, the illustrations of his arch and his roasted ox, the praises of the diners. Such publicity, such glory, such applause were better than any amount of money.

When beginning to plan the Great Exhibition of 1851 Prince Albert and the Lord Mayor of London had invited all the provincial mayors to a great banquet in London. 'In their turn', wrote Soyer, 'the mayors of Great Britain and Ireland were desirous of offering to the Lord Mayor of the city of London a banquet at which his Royal Highness would be present; and this feast, a grandiose and sympathetic demonstration on the part of the votaries of the London Exhibition, took place the 25th October, 1850, in the Gothic Guildhall of York, where remembrance of the past was blended with hopes of the future. It was resolved to entrust us with the direction of the gastronomic department, and, let us add, the artistic arrangement of the banquet, which, by reason of its unprecedented richness and truly magic aspect, no pen can describe, owing partly to the magnificence of the maces, swords, banners, etc. of each county being for the first time displayed under the same roof.' *Partly*—and partly, we are left to infer, to the genius of the hand which arranged them!

The decorations, with which Soyer had an entirely free hand, were indeed remarkable, elaborate and overwhelming. In engravings of the royal table, glimpses of the principal guests are caught as they peer out from the jungle of urns, vases, statues and lamps, epergnes and plateaux and centre-pieces heaped with mountains of fruit[1] and pyramids of flowers, which the *chef* had piled in front of them.

'The most conspicuous ornament'—to quote its designer —'was a large emblematic vase, twenty feet in height.' He was extremely proud of this creation. 'Around the base are Europe, Asia, Africa and America, presenting specimens of

---

[1] The most striking fruits were 'two magnificent pines from Chatsworth, weighing nearly fifteen pounds each'—a variety called by Paxton 'Royal Providence'.

industry to Britannia. From the centre of the base springs a palm tree, surrounded by the arms of the cities of London and York; medallion portraits of Her Majesty and Prince Albert, encircled by the shields of the principal cities and towns of the United Kingdom, form the body of the vase; two figures of Ireland and Scotland the handles; the Prince of Wales's emblem the neck, and the royal arms the apex. Appended were graceful wreaths of flowers, in which the symbols of the Houses of York and Lancaster (red and white roses) predominated; and when a brilliant flood of gaslight, added to by powerful reflectors, was thrown upon this splendid decoration, the effect was truly magnificent.' It is not astonishing that Prince Albert 'appeared to be much struck with the remarkable coup d'œil'.[1]

L'Extravagance Culinaire à l'Alderman

In the body of the hall two hundred and forty-eight guests were served with a magnificent feast, and the eighteen who sat at the royal table had a still finer collection of dishes offered to them. Exclusive of wines, the dinner cost six

[1] *The Illustrated London News.*

hundred pounds. Many dishes were appropriately *à la
Victoria*, *à la Prince of Wales*, *à la Albert* and even *à la Lady
Mayoress*, but the most extraordinary creation, the 'hundred-
guinea dish', was entitled *L'Extravagance Culinaire à l'Alderman*. 'The opportunity of producing some gastronomic phe-
nomenon for the royal table...was irresistible', Soyer
confessed; 'accordingly the following *choice morsels* were
carefully selected from all the birds mentioned in the bill of
fare, to form a dish of delicacies worthy of his Royal Highness
and the noble guests around him. The extravagance of this
dish, valued at one hundred guineas, is accounted for by
supposing that if an epicure were to order a similar one for a
small party, he would be obliged to provide:

		£	s.	d.
5	Turtle heads, part of fins and green fat	34	0	0
24	Capons, the two small *noix* from each side of the middle of the back only used, being the most delicate part of every bird	8	8	0
18	Turkeys, the same	8	12	0
18	Fatted Pullets, the same	5	17	0
16	Fowls, the same	2	8	0
10	Grouse	2	5	0
20	Pheasants, *noix* only	3	0	0
45	Partridges, the same	3	7	0
6	Plovers, whole		9	0
100	Snipes, *noix* only	5	0	0
36	Quails, whole	3	0	0
40	Woodcocks, *noix* only	8	0	0
36	Pigeons, the same		14	0
72	Larks, stuffed		15	0
	Ortolans from Belgium	5	0	0
	The *garniture*, consisting of cockscombs, truffles, mushrooms, crawfish, olives, American asparagus, *croustades* (paste crust), sweetbreads, *quenelles de volaille* (strips or slices of fowl), green mangoes, and a new sauce	14	10	0
		105	5	0

Soyer enjoyed the whole affair enormously, but was sometimes
annoyed by the familiarity of a group of young clerks, who

managed to scrape acquaintance with him and hung round
him at all hours of the day. One of them slapped him on the
back, saying, 'I'll tell you what, Soyer, you are a regular
brick!'—'I'll tell *you* what, then,' cried the exasperated *chef*,
'you are the mortar that sticks to the brick.'

After the dinner Soyer gave a great supper to everyone
who had helped him, and returned to London next day, again
out of pocket, but rich in new friendships and a fresh blaze
of glory.

CHAPTER X

THE GASTRONOMIC SYMPOSIUM
OF ALL NATIONS

'It was a miracle of rare device,
A sunny pleasure-dome with caves of ice!'

COLERIDGE, *Kubla Khan*

In the autumn of 1850 George Augustus Sala and his brother
were walking through Hungerford Market when they noticed
a man bargaining for lobsters. 'Who can that extraordinary
individual be?' George asked his brother. He goes on, 'The
stranger was a stoutish, tallish gentleman, a little past middle
age, with closely cropped grey hair and a stubbly grey
moustache; and, but for his more than peculiar costume, he
might have been mistaken for the riding-master of a foreign
circus, who had been originally in the army. He wore a kind
of paletot of light camlet cloth, with voluminous lapels and
deep cuffs of lavender watered silk; very baggy trousers, with
lavender stripes down the seams; very shiny boots and quite
as glossy a hat; his attire being completed by tightly-fitting
gloves of light yellow. An extraordinary oddity was added
to his appearance by the circumstance that every article of his
attire, save I suppose his gloves and boots, was cut on what
dressmakers call a "bias", or as he himself, when I came to
know him well, used to designate as *à la zoug-zoug*....

'He evidently knew all about shellfish...and offered terms
for them...which were at length, and not very ruefully,
accepted by the fishmonger, who was possibly desirous of
keeping on the best of terms with the foreign gentleman
whose hat, coat, cravat and pantaloons were all so studiously
awry. "Who is that?" said my brother, repeating my
question. "Why, of all people, who could it be but Soyer?
How do you do, Soyer."'

The *chef* invited the brothers to sup with him, and struck up a warm friendship with George Augustus, who on his part was first attracted by Soyer's wit and eccentricity, and then charmed by his good humour and generosity. Sala became for a time Soyer's confidant, secretary and right-hand man, and enthusiastically supported the *chef's* new venture—a restaurant to feed visitors to the Great Exhibition of 1851.

The Committee of the Exhibition had invited tenders for supplying refreshments within the Crystal Palace, but the restrictions were so many that Soyer had hardly considered applying for the official contract. Three refreshment rooms were to be organised, of different classes—and equal inadequacy. Each was to supply only 'light and moderate refreshments' and lest they should 'assume the character of an hotel, tavern or dining-rooms', no drink stronger than gingerbeer was to be served; indeed, the contractor was bound to supply 'fresh filtered water in glasses gratis to visitors'. No cooking might be done on the premises, and it was even suggested that visitors ought to consume such food as was allowed them standing up.

Since it was to be so uncomfortable to eat and quite impossible to drink within the building, and since exhibitions are of all things the most exhausting, a comfortable restaurant close to the Crystal Palace seemed certain to be a success. A friend offered to supply the necessary capital if Soyer would act as manager; on condition that he should have a free hand with the arrangement and decoration of the building, and of course complete dominion over the kitchens, Soyer agreed to become a partner. A lease was taken of Gore House, only a few hundred yards from the Exhibition.

When Soyer was already committed to these plans, he was surprised to get a letter from the Exhibition Committee:

Sir,—If it is at all your intention to tender for the refreshments at the Exhibition, and you think it advisable to have *single* glasses of wine served, will you be kind enough to mention such wish in your tender?

Though flattered by the indirect invitation, Soyer realised that it was impossible to run two establishments at once, and since he much preferred to be entirely his own master, he thanked the committee but refused to tender. Eventually, Messrs Schweppes won the contract with a bid of five thousand pounds, and sold food to the value of £75,557. 15s. 0d. to 6,039,135 people. This included 1,804,718 buns (934,691 Bath buns and 870,027 plain), also 1,092,337 bottles of soda-water, lemonade and gingerbeer at sixpence a glass. The exhibitors alone consumed 1046 gallons of pickles.

The work of replanning Gore House was more exciting than the earlier designing of the kitchens of the Reform Club. Then Soyer had been, it is true, an expert and technical adviser, but the last word had always been with the committee or the architect; now he was a veritable Pooh Bah—Architect, Engineer, Designer, Landscape Gardener, Decorator, Plumber, and Lord High Everything Else. Whole-heartedly as ever he plunged into the maze of alteration, improvement and reconstruction; as ever, financial considerations were forgotten as he planned splendour upon splendour and glory upon glory; by the time he left London to complete a provincial tour with the Magic Stove, an army of workmen—'carpenters, scene-painters, plumbers, glaziers, gardeners, town-travellers for ironmongers, wine-merchants and drapers, upholsterers, carvers, gilders'—armed with his detailed instructions, were in possession of Gore House. In March the tour ended; Soyer returned to London and took up residence in his new restaurant, which he re-christened in honour of the International Exhibition, THE GASTRONOMIC SYMPOSIUM OF ALL NATIONS.

'From all quarters of the globe, civilised or uncivilised', said the catalogue, 'will his visitors come—the doors of the Symposium will be thrown open to universal humanity.' 'Cosmopolitan customs', it went on, 'should demand cosmopolitan cooking'; Frenchmen were promised fricandeaux, Turks pillaf and hachis, Persians sherbert, Spaniards olla

102

podrida, Americans johnny-cakes and canvas-back ducks; Chinese were to have stewed dog, Russians caviar, Cossacks train oil, Tartars mare's milk, New Zealanders—but no, even Soyer had his limits, 'No, not New Zealanders, for who could form any idea of the horror and dismay which would be caused by some ebony-skinned and boomeranged chieftain demanding "baked young woman for two" and a "cold boiled missionary" to follow?'

Gore House was a long low building, faced with white stucco, lying a little back from the road and screened by high walls and great gates. In the gardens pear and fig trees clung to the old red brick walls, white and purple lilacs bloomed by the terrace, and the flower beds were full of roses; among green lawns and shady walks stood great clumps of old mulberries and walnuts.

Perhaps the most magnificent room was the library, which stretched the full length of the house from north to south. The books which had lined the walls were gone, but the panels of the doors and the spaces between the shelves were still filled with mirrors, while at each end there were elaborately carved marble fireplaces, and in the centre delicate marble columns supported an arch. It had been the scene of Lady Blessington's famous gatherings, to which all the town—writers, politicians, poets, actors, painters and musicians—had flocked. 'Where else', asked Landor, 'can I find so much wit, so much wisdom?'

Everyone who was anyone visited Gore House, but its great rooms, magnificent gardens and abundant hospitality could not be kept up on a jointure of a thousand a year. Lady Blessington's debts accumulated, while those of her son-in-law d'Orsay reached an enormous figure. While the élite gossiped in the library, duns hammered at the gates, and for years d'Orsay dared not go out by daylight. In 1849 the crash came. Lady Blessington fled to Paris, and the contents of the house were sold.

George Augustus Sala had published in 1850 a booklet of cartoons entitled *The Great Exhibition Wot is to Be*, containing hundreds of figures with large heads and tiny bodies going in procession to the Exhibition. Americans were pictured drinking sherry-cobblers, beating their slaves, waving six-shooters, and swinging in rocking-chairs; Italians ate macaroni and ground barrel-organs; Spaniards danced the cachucha; Irishmen and Turks and Jews and African savages were all appropriately described and employed. The author later described it as a 'farrago of juvenile impertinence'.

In the French section, near Dumas hauling a trolley-load of his works, Rachel as Phèdre, and Victor Hugo with a model of Notre-Dame, Soyer was shown. In one hand he grasped a saucepan, in the other his Magic Stove, and behind him stood enormous copies of his *Gastronomic Regenerator* and his *Modern Housewife*. The inscription below ran: 'French Cooking in the Person of M. Soyer and his Books. Air: "Why, oh why, did Soyer resign?"'

Soyer thought the whole booklet extremely amusing, was flattered by his own inclusion, and commissioned Sala to paint on the grand staircase of the Symposium a somewhat similar panorama, containing every celebrity, real or mythological, who could be crowded in. They were all rushing upwards, some on foot, some on hippogrifs, griffins, giraffes, scorpions, mice, elephants, mastodons, dragons, and every other possible mount. Pitt was there, and his enemy Fox, Wellington was not far from Napoleon, Brougham and Ali Baba, Thiers and Minerva, Guizot, Dickens, Mark Lemon, George Cruikshank, Thackeray, Balfe, Jerrold, Dumas, General Tom Thumb, Jullien the musician, Victor Hugo, John Bright, Cobden, and many more, with mobs of unidentified Indians and Esquimaux and savages.

Soyer insisted on having this panorama called 'The Grand Macédoine of all Nations, being a Demisemitragicomigrotesquepanofanofanifunnisymposiorama, or Such-a-getting-upstairs-to-the-Great-Exhibition-of-1851'. 'I groaned', wrote

Sala, 'as I interpolated this hideous rubbish in my manuscript'
—he was writing the *catalogue raisonné*. The artist's pride was
hurt, and he revenged himself by calling Soyer 'nothing if not
fantastic, and to a certain extent quackish'.

The programme[1] was printed 'on satin paper, the edges
delicately printed green and scalloped', and it promised every
sort of refreshment in every sort of room, from the Blessington
Temple of the Muses—a gallery divided by Ionic pilasters in
white and gold, with panelled recesses filled with white
drapery fluted with green; with a profusion of plate glass,
a ceiling representing a genial summer sky, and brackets
supporting pots of flowers—to the Baronial Banqueting Hall,
erected in the gardens, the outside like 'a time-worn Gothic
donjon, a pile of castellated masonry such as we see pictur-
esquely rising from the blue waters of the Rhine', while inside
the roof was of stained glass and the walls were covered with
crimson drapery, any spaces being filled alternately with
Emma's works and blazons of the insignia of various countries;
there was also a complete collection of crayon portraits by
Count d'Orsay. At one end was erected the symbolic vase
which had been designed for the great dinner at York.[2]

Extra ground was bought, enclosed, named the *Pré d'Orsay*,
and adorned with 'grassy pyramids supporting vases of
flowers and Watteau-like statues'. Here was built the Monster
Pavilion of All Nations (in which fifteen hundred people
could dine at once) four hundred feet in length, with an
enormous tablecloth ('of British manufacture') three hundred
and seven feet long. 'A splendid collation was here provided
each day for those who preferred the promiscuous refection of
a public banquet to the more select yet less joyous society of
a private room.' The grounds were transformed. There was
'a sloping terrace of flowers in the form of a gigantic shell,
crammed with choicest roses' which people came to admire
again and again.

[1] See Appendix D for prospectus.
[2] See pp. 96–7.

Inside, Gore House was altered out of recognition. Well might *Punch* write 'To M. Soyer, on his "Symposium"':

> Soyer, the praise thy skill deserves
> > Is perfectly immense,
> For nice discernment in the nerves
> > Of gustatory sense;
>
> But now Gore House hath been by thee
> > So glaringly defaced,
> However good thy palate be
> > We must dispute thy taste.

'In honest truth', Sala admitted years later, 'we had played the very dickens with it.' There was, however, something magnificent in the lengths to which Soyer's fantasy could go, something impressive in his gargantuan imaginings, something almost awe-inspiring in the amazing excesses of his bad taste, and perhaps something pathetic in the immense pride he felt for his creations.

In the Hall of Architectural Wonders the visitors saw St Peter's, the Tower of Pisa, the Duomo of Milan, the Louvre, the lion of St Mark, the Mosque of St Sophia, the Pyramids, Pompey's Pillar, the Porcelain Tower of Nankin, the Bridge of Sighs, the Sphinx, the Eddystone Lighthouse, St Paul's, the Monument, and—among many more—'the new palace of Westminster, and that latest triumph of combined engineering skill and artistic beauty, the Tubular Bridge.' And the visitors loved it. 'If the unities of architectural decorum were lost sight of', said a critic, 'an ensemble was produced of a pleasing and novel character.'

From the French windows of the grand salon the visitor stepped out on to the Banqueting Bridge ('decidedly Italian') from which a double stair led down to the gardens. Beneath the bridge was the Transatlantic Antechamber (or Washington Refreshment Room), supplying 'every kind of American beverage', where the walls were decorated with stars and stripes. The gorgeous *Boudoir de la Vallière* had a ceiling which seemed 'a Chinese puzzle of fluted white and blue satin,

M. Soyer's Symposium (from *The Illustrated London News*)

heightened with silver, while the walls presented a curious, yet a beautiful, pattern of zig-zag stripes, and broad diagonal bands of black velvet and silver lace'.

Soyer's ceilings were characteristic. In *La Salle de Noces de Danae* the ceiling was 'an elaborate and gorgeously tinted specimen of perforated arabesque, its open lattice-work answering admirably for ventilation, and constructed on a plan never before attempted'. (Notice the mixture of the practical and the fantastic, and the insistence on the novelty of his work.) 'It united the graceful scroll-work and richness of detail of the Renaissance to the delicate and fancifully elegant tracery of the Alhambra. The prevailing colour was pale green *parsemé* with many-hued flowers, and profusely enriched with gold, while through its perforations were visible the clear blue tints of a summer sky. Showers of tears of embossed gold and silver left the cornice. . . .'

In the garden a pavilion of many-coloured stalactites had a ceiling and double windows of crystal, with gold and silver fish appearing through them. This grotto was surmounted with a statue of Hebe, who 'from her enchanted cup, dispensed to mortals through the shafts of the temple artfully concocted liqueurs'.

Then an army of pages, cooks, scullions, waiters, barmaids and clerks of the kitchen were engaged, Soyer choosing the smartest little boys with the curliest hair, and barmaids and waitresses so pretty that they were described as a beauty chorus.

When all was finished, even to the arch of camelias in *La Cabinet de Toilette à la Pompadour* and the arctic fox crouching in its burrow in *La Grotte des Neiges Éternelles*, Soyer held a series of private views, lasting a fortnight. It soon became known that the *chef, capable du tout*, had surpassed even his own previous extravagances, and everyone wanted to see the Symposium. The Russian ambassador was among the earliest visitors; Wellington came back to dine several times after his first visit of inspection; Mr Lumley of Her Majesty's was so struck by the staircase that he put Sala on his free list for the season, and Fox and Henderson, who had built the Crystal Palace, came to inspect the 'rival wonder'. Disraeli presented Soyer with a quotation from one of his novels; it was printed on white watered silk, with a gold fringe, and contained an allusion to the Beautiful— whether in compliment or rebuke is not known.

A big visitors' book, 'blazing with gold and morocco,' lay in the library, and exhibited an amazing collection of names. The Duchess of Sutherland's signature appeared beside that of Madame St Leon (once Fanny Cerito); 'Jules Janin's name', wrote Sala, 'came close to the laborious *paraphe* of an eminent pugilist. Members of the American congress found themselves in juxtapositions with Frederick Douglass, and the dark gentleman who came as Ambassador from Hayti. I remember one Sunday seeing Mr Disraeli, the author of *Vanity Fair*, a privy councillor, a Sardinian attaché, the Marquis of Normanby, the late Mr Flexmore the clown, the editor of *Punch*, the Wizard of the North, all pressing to enter the whilom boudoir of the Blessington.'

Thackeray brought 'Dicky' Doyle of *Punch*, and in the garden they met their host. Proudly he showed them the enormous tent where the half-crown dinners were to be served. 'Zis', he said, 'is ze Baronial Hall.' 'I should rather have thought', cried Thackeray, 'that it was a marquee!' Thackeray was so amused by the Symposium that he gave his 'esteemed friend, the regenerator' some most valuable publicity, devoting two long articles in *Punch* to the *chef* and his restaurant. They were written as if literally translated from the French, and signed by 'Gobemouche, Man of Letters, Man of Taste'.

The first is about 'The French Conspiration', and admits frankly that the French mean to conquer England. But their leader is no mere soldier—he is Alexis Soyer. 'Is not the man of all England the most admired and beloved a Frenchman? Whose name, whose good things are in so many people's

mouths as the name, as the good things of ALEXIS SOYER?'
And so, after much personal praise, on to Gore House. 'A
palace of fairies is he making of it—truly a Symposium of All
Nations.... You may consume here the cockaliquet of the
mountains of Scotland, the garbanzos of Castile, the shamrock
of Ireland, the macaroni of Vesuvius, the kari of the Ganges
and the cabob of the Bosphorus; you may here call for the
golden juice of the Rhine and the purple draught of the
Garonne, as for the whiski of the Liffi and the Afandaf (liquor
which I adore) of the Thames. SIR SOYER will soon be prepared to furnish you with all these.... This, Milord, is the
Conspiracy by which France hopes to conquer you—this is
the representative which the Republic sends to Albion.'

A month later there appeared 'M. Gobemouche's Authentic
Account of the Grand Exhibition'. Gobemouche told his cab
driver to conduct him to the Palace of All Nations. He
describes his amazement and wonder as he wandered from
room to room and from hall to hall, each decorated in the
style of a different people. In the lovely park outside he saw
a vast building with 'battlemented walls and transparent
roof'—here, he decided, was the 'much-vaunted Palace of
Crystal'. '"That is the Baronial Hall of All Nations", said a
gentleman to me—a gentleman in a flowing robe and a singular
cap, whom I had mistaken for a Chinese or an enchanter.... I
pause. I muse. I meditate. Where have I seen that face?
Where noted that mien, that cap? Ah, I have it!—in the
books devoted to gastronomic regeneration, on the flasks of
sauce called relish. This is not the Crystal Palace I see—this
is the rival wonder—yes, this is the Symposium of All
Nations, and yonder man is ALEXIS SOYER!'

On 15th May a grand dinner was served 'to the Literati of
All Nations'—in other words, to some three hundred foreign
writers, journalists and artists then visiting the Great Exhibition. They were shown over the Symposium, and were
duly impressed and astonished at the sight of a baron of beef
being roasted in the open air by gas. When cooked, it was

played into the Baronial Hall to the tune of 'The Roast Beef of Old England', and the feast began. 'Description now becomes hopeless', declared the *Morning Chronicle*, 'imagination may do something, but experience alone can convey an idea adequate to the occasion.' They were given, according to *The Times*, 'all the good things that the combination of art and nature can produce.'

The visitors came from every corner of the world—Paris, Dresden, Havana, Leipsic, St Petersburg, Amsterdam, Frankfort, Dublin—and the band played the *Marseillaise, Yankee-Doodle, God Save the Queen* and any other national airs they knew, quite impartially throughout the meal. Soyer's health was drunk with musical honours, and he responded with much emotion, hoping that the patronage he had always had given him so freely in England would not cease, 'now that', he said, 'I have engaged in more extended operations—now that like Caesar I have crossed the Rubicon, and unfurled the banner of gastronomy, not only to a nation, but to the world.' (Loud cheering.) He went on to dilate on his favourite project, 'the establishment of a national school of scientific and economical domestic cookery' (great applause), and declared that as soon as the Symposium was well established he would start a model school of cookery within its walls.

But this time Soyer had—if the gastronomic metaphor is permissible—bitten off more than he could chew. He had squandered money recklessly upon his fantastic decorations, and his partners were uneasy. The whole affair had been so hurriedly planned that—unlike all his earlier ventures—there was a good deal of waste and inefficiency. The private meals, prepared to order, were always irreproachably cooked and served, but no one man could supervise every meal in so vast an establishment, and sometimes there were complaints about the shilling dinners.

On the whole, however, visitors felt that they were getting more than their money's worth. After they had eaten they could wander through the house and gardens, which were amazing in themselves, or listen to the musicians and singers whom Soyer engaged. Among the most popular of these were the Ethiopian Serenaders, who since their first concerts in England in 1846 had become very much the rage. A sybil told fortunes in the Gipsy Dell, and towards the end of the summer balloon ascents were made from the gardens every afternoon.

One well-pleased guest suggested an epigram by Martial as motto for the Symposium:

> Dic quotus es, quanti cupias cenare, nec unum
> Addideris verbum: cena parata tibi est.

> Say how many you are, and at what cost you wish to dine;
> Add not a word—your dinner is arranged.

This was in fact the plan followed by wise visitors, who knew that if they told Soyer they wished to dine, say, four friends at seven shillings each, and left the rest to him, they would get a better dinner than any of their own designing. Delighted by the implied compliment, Soyer had the couplet painted over the entrance.

Nearly all of the visitors to the Symposium were people coming on from the Crystal Palace, and it was clear that if the restaurant was to remain open after the Exhibition closed, some other attractions must be added to it. Soyer could not bear the idea of closing his beloved Gore House, and persuaded Jullien, the popular musician and impresario, to join him in building a winter garden in the grounds, where concerts and even dances might be held.

Jullien was the son of a Paris bandmaster, and though he did not distinguish himself at the Conservatoire, he had an immense success when he came over to England in 1840. He started shilling 'concerts d'été' at Drury Lane, which were so popular that he progressed in 1841 to 'concerts d'hiver' and in 1842 to 'concerts de société', and the series continued yearly till 1859. In 1844 he was turning out a new polka every fortnight, but he always kept before him his ideal 'to popularise good music'; in each programme he included 'one piece of acknowledged eminence'—often a movement of a symphony—sandwiched between popular airs of the day.

Every year he composed a topical 'Monster Quadrille'— English and French and Royal Irish Quadrilles, a Crystal Fountain Polka in 1851, an Allied Armies Quadrille in 1854, and an Indian Quadrille, including Havelock's *March*, in the year of the Mutiny.[1]

Like Soyer, Jullien demanded the best of everything to do with his art; he brought to England not only the best players for his orchestra, but the best soloists and the best singers. Again like Soyer, he planned on a grandiose scale; he often conducted an orchestra of ninety with a chorus of eighty, and for some of his compositions used his whole orchestra combined with no less than six military bands.

The public loved him. Whether his fortunes were up or down—he was often in trouble from too-ambitious undertakings—their affection and interest were unchanged. M. Jullien—'the Mons.', as *Punch* christened him—was the delight of the cartoonists also. He dressed most elaborately for his performances; his embroidered shirt frills stuck out over a spotless white waistcoat, his enormous wristbands were turned back over his cuffs, and he conducted dramatically—in fact, melodramatically. His baton waved with ever-increasing passion, his coat tails swung violently; at the climax he would seize a violin or piccolo and play and conduct as well, and finally sink back exhausted into his gorgeous velvet chair, until the thunderous applause of the audience brought him back to his feet, his beaming face crowned by its wealth of

[1] 'Who now remembers gay Cremorne
    And all its jaunty jills,
And those wild whirling figures born
    Of Jullien's grand quadrilles?
With hats on head and morning coats
There footed to his prancing notes
    Our partner girls and we....'

pomaded curls, and his enormous jet-black moustachios posi-
tively bristling with excitement. For Beethoven, he always
used a special jewelled baton, held in a pair of white kid
gloves ostentatiously handed to him on a silver salver.

With all his absurdities and affectations, Jullien performed
a very real service to music in England. By insisting on the
best players, he raised the general standard of performance,
and by slipping a movement of a Beethoven or Mozart
symphony into a popular programme, he gradually accustomed the public to better music, until towards the end of
his career he was including a whole symphony, or sometimes
even two, in each programme. He and Soyer were a well-
matched pair, alike in their outward extravagances and their
inward sincerity; also alike, unfortunately, in their boundless
optimism and in the lack of business sense which made them
embark on immense schemes without the necessary backing.
They decided to join in the building of a music-hall at Gore
House, and applied for a licence.

As well as feeding individual visitors to the Exhibition,
Soyer provided dinners at Gore House for large parties of
excursionists and for various societies and clubs. Some of
these banquets were most respectable affairs, as that of 'the
members and friends of the Metropolitan Sanitary Associa-
tion', when Charles Dickens was one of the principal speakers.
Others were more rowdy. One evening towards the end of
the summer a party of two hundred country people, led by
their parson, were given dinner in the Encampment of All
Nations, after an exciting day at the Exhibition. After dining
they spread all over the house and grounds, dancing to the
music, drinking at the various bars, and thoroughly enjoying
themselves. As there were the usual four or five hundred
other people also enjoying themselves, the place was crowded,
and there was a great deal of confused merriment and
noise.

Unfortunately, this was the evening chosen by Mr Pownall,
chairman of the Middlesex Sessions, for a visit to Gore House,

that he might decide whether the licence for the Symposium (obtained the year before after many difficulties) should or should not be renewed. The crowd, the noise, the gaiety horrified him. Soyer heard that the licence would certainly not be renewed, and when the case was called at the Sessions did not appear; but Mr Pownall would not let the matter drop. He had, he said, 'paid the Symposium a visit, and a more dissipated place, or a more dangerous place for the morals of young persons, he had never entered. He had never been a witness to such disgraceful dissipation in his life.'

To Soyer, passionately proud of his name and his reputation, this was a thunderbolt. He was furiously angry. Without consulting his partners, he shut the Symposium abruptly on 14th October. He wrote indignantly to the press, demanding of 'the public who have visited Gore House if they can corroborate any such attack upon me or upon the respectability of my establishment. I have', he went on, 'above two thousand autographs of the élite of society of all nations, who have visited Gore House repeatedly, and who have always spoken most highly of the manner in which it was conducted. I am proud to say that on the very night that gentleman [Mr Pownall] paid me a visit, several of the nobility were there dining and spending the evening, and expressed to me the highest approbation of the arrangements.' He mentioned with regret the 'magnificent *jardin d'hiver et d'été*' which he and Jullien had planned, and declared that he was taking legal proceedings against Mr Pownall, 'as the only means of vindicating my character, and that of above a hundred servants dependent on me, whom the remarks of Mr Pownall are calculated to ruin'.

The sudden closing of Gore House caused some alarm among Soyer's creditors, though a notice invited those who had claims to apply at Messrs Soyer and Company's offices for full payment. A few creditors started legal proceedings to recover their money, but they might have saved themselves the trouble, for in a month or so Soyer had settled all his accounts.

Strictly honourable, he used all his savings and the royalties on his books to pay his debts, and told Sala that he was left with barely one hundred pounds. During the five months of its existence, visitors had spent in the Symposium the large sum of twenty-one thousand pounds, but money had been squandered recklessly on decorations and buildings, and the expenses had been twenty-eight thousand.

Soyer could never understand his losses at Gore House. He had worked early and late, he had created what he considered to be the most beautiful and original of restaurants, over a thousand people had been served—to their great satisfaction—daily, and what had come of it all? He had lost seven thousand pounds, and, what he minded far more, his good name had been attacked and his reputation temporarily clouded.

The Great Exhibition made a profit of a hundred and eighty-six thousand pounds, and the committee for some unfathomable reason decided that it should be spent on 'museums and galleries'. Gore House and twenty-two acres of ground were purchased with part of the money, and on the site of the Symposium now stands the Albert Hall.

While Soyer was still at Gore House, he found one day among his letters one from Paris, in a strange hand. He tore it open in his usual impetuous way, talking all the time of the day's business, but when he had read a few lines, he became silent and absorbed, finished it with close attention, and was obviously much distressed. He left his work, and going to his old friend Volant said, 'Read this, old boy', then putting a forefinger across his lips added, 'Let me know what you think of it.'

Volant saw tears in his friend's eyes, and glanced quickly through the letter. 'Sir—forgive me if I am bold enough to write these few lines...born in Paris...without knowing of my father...my dear mother Adèle Lamain...anxious to know who I was...succeeded in learning the name...seeing

your address in the newspapers...thought of starting for
England...permission to join you...the friendship which a
father cannot help granting to his son...do not refuse me....'

Volant could not believe his eyes. It seemed impossible
that Soyer, who with all his eccentricity was one of the kindest,
most affectionate and most generous of men, should have
deserted and forgotten a mistress and her child when he came
to England. Soyer himself was even more astounded. Adèle
Lamain was an almost forgotten ghost of his youth, he had
never known that she had a child—still less that it was his.
However, dates, places and names seemed plausible, and
Soyer's curiosity alone, apart from all the other emotions
stirred by the letter, would not let him rest. The writer was
invited to come to the Symposium.

Father and son were delighted with each other. Soyer's
high spirits and overflowing energy made him more like a
brother than a father, and young Alexis remained for a
fortnight, seeing the Symposium, the Exhibition and London
under his father's guidance, and meeting all his father's
friends—though they were not told who the young man
was.

After he had returned to Paris, to the uncle who had
brought him up, young Alexis kept in touch with Soyer, and
wrote often to Volant, begging him to persuade Soyer to give
his son his name. In 1853 Soyer visited Alexis in Paris, and
decided to acknowledge him as his son. Alexis Lamain
became Alexis Soyer, and wrote to Volant of his joy when at
last he could 'add next to the Christian name of Alexis the
glorious one of Soyer'.

In 1911 a craze for ' paper-bag cookery' swept over England;
its chief exponent was one Nicolas Soyer, who boasted that
he was the grandson of ' the great Soyer, whose name is known
to *chefs* the world over'. Like his grandfather, Nicolas was
brought up in France and destined for the Church, but became
a cook who went to England and was *chef* to several of the

nobility and gentry. Nicolas too was for a time *chef* to a famous club—in his case Brooks's.

Boosted by the *Daily Chronicle*, paper-bag cookery became the rage, and the praises of Soyer's paper-bags were sung in much the same accents that had once greeted his grandfather's magic stove. 'In the depths of the lonely valley,' wrote George R. Sims, 'on the summit of the cloud-capped mountains, among the eternal snows, and on the sand-swept deserts the traveller with a supply of Soyer bags will be able to cook a meal that may be to many a wandering son of Britain a sunny souvenir of the Savoy, and a radiant reminiscence of the Ritz.' Though this prophecy was hardly justified, yet friends of Nicolas declared that he had many of his grandfather's qualities, 'the same high appreciation of his art, the same inventive genius, the same passion for organisation, the same magnetic personality.'

To read Nicolas's books is to be irresistibly reminded of his grandfather's—' Often I would get up at two in the morning in order that I might put my paper bag to some fresh test'— 'Expert cooking, which has hitherto been the luxury of the RICH, can now be equally the privilege of the POOR'—'I do not claim for the paper-bag system of cookery that it can cook everything. It is evident that the national beverage must still be cooked in the tea-pot.' In every phrase there is an echo of Alexis.

CHAPTER XI

THE YEARS 1851-4

'And I said, "Oh gentle pieman, why so very, very merry?
Is it purity of conscience, or your one-and-seven sherry?"

But he answered, "I'm so happy—no profession could be dearer—
If I'm not humming 'Tra! la! la!' I'm singing 'Tirer lirer!'

First I go and make the patties and the puddings and the jellies,
Then I make a sugar bird-cage which upon a table swell is;

Then I polish all the silver which a supper table lacquers,
Then I write the pretty mottoes which you find inside the crackers".'

GILBERT, *Ferdinando and Elvira*

WHEN Soyer left the Reform Club a wise friend had advised him to 'take a house and give therein, without any claptrap show or external demonstration, *the best dinners* that a man could get in London'. Disregarding this, Soyer had plunged into the adventure of Gore House, which instead of making him famous and rich had left him notorious and almost penniless. His adviser wrote lamenting: 'Had you followed my advice, you would have made your fortune....The world had faith in Soyer, and you might have dictated your own terms. If you will set about repairing past mischief at once, keep yourself in your own hands, take a quiet place, cook the very best dinners, give the very best wines, people will still go to Soyer. But I warn you as you value your respectability and credit, to avoid anything that has the remotest resemblance to puff and charlatanism; you stand in need of neither, and may get on very well without them.'

Admirable advice—for anyone but Alexis Soyer. Publicity was to him like hunting to Jorrocks—'It is like the hair we breathe. If we 'ave it not we die.'

His pet idea—a college or school of domestic economy—had to be rejected because of lack of capital. He was next

119

asked by the proprietor of the Hall of Commerce in the City to open it as an eating-house, also available for banquets. Soyer at once envisioned the hall fitted up as a Paris restaurant, with clients lounging in comfortable chairs at elegant little tables, eating the best of food, both French and English. The dining-hall would be hung with his wife's pictures, and the service would be entirely French. He imagined masses of flowers, long vistas of looking-glasses, and handsomely dressed female cashiers. In short, a 'Corner House' of the nineteen-thirties.

But City men in the eighteen-fifties wanted no more for lunch than their chop or steak or cut off the joint, served as quickly as possible; they did not object to the greasy waiters, the narrow, cushionless stalls, the sawdust-covered floors, the dirty tablecloths, the dubious cutlery and the complete lack of ventilation which characterised almost every City eating-house at the time.[1] Luncheon was the only meal served at restaurants; even in the eighteen-sixties few people of *ton* would eat in public, and the City men whom Soyer hoped to attract hurried home at night to dine in the midst of the family circle. Soyer was persuaded to abandon the idea, and for the next three years he launched no grand scheme, though he was fully occupied with a hundred smaller matters.

At the end of 1851 a very unsavoury scandal was exposed, when the preserved meats supplied to the navy began literally to stink in the public's nostrils. Complaints were made at Gosport about appalling smells, which were traced to canisters

[1] Cf. Mr Jorrocks (*Handley Cross*) in 1854: 'Now for a chop-house or coffee-room dinner! Oh the 'orrible smell that greets you at the door! Compound of cabbage, pickled salmon, boiled beef, sawdust and anchovy sarce. "Wot will you take, sir?", inquires the frowsty waiter, smoothin' the filthy, mustardy, cabbagey cloth, "soles, macrel, vitin's —werry good boiled beef—nice cut, cabbage, cold 'am and weal, cold lamb and sallard."—Hah! The den's 'ot to suffocation—the kitchen's below—a trap-door womits up dinners in return for bellows down the pipe to the cook. Flies settle on your face—swarm on your head; a wasp travels around; everything tastes flat, stale and unprofitable.'

of meat in the Government stores. On investigation 5468 cans out of 6378 were found to be full of 'garbage and putridity in a horrible state' and those that were well enough preserved for the contents to be identifiable were found to contain 'offal and carrion'. They were taken out and sunk off Spithead where, the sailors said, they killed an uncommon lot of fishes.

The indignant public demanded an enquiry, and Soyer was asked to report on the whole question of preserving meat for long voyages. Evidently the failure of Gore House had not affected his credit seriously, for the columns of the *Lancet* were flung open for his conclusions, which he gave at great length; various alterations were made as he advised.

Free from regular working hours, Soyer spent even more time than before on charitable work, superintending the running and improvement of soup-kitchens in Ham Yard and Leicester Square. To get funds to support them, he organised a grand ball in Willis's Rooms, at which the *beau monde* danced to Jullien's band, and between dances watched Soyer exhibit all the newest methods of cooking by gas. In Ham Yard a Christmas dinner was served to twenty-two thousand of the poorest of the poor,[1] the *pièce de résistance* of the feast being Soyer's old favourite, an ox roasted whole by gas. Knowing that it was not enough to feed the body alone, he engaged a band to play during the dinner, and knives and forks moved briskly to the 'waltzes, polkas and merry tunes' which were performed.

In 1853 he designed the City Soup Kitchen in Farringdon Street, which was opened with great *éclat* by the Lord Mayor, and supplied eight to ten thousand people every day.

With all this care for those who ate to live, he did not forget those who lived to eat. He was for ever experimenting with condiments, and invented an aromatic mustard which became one of Crosse and Blackwell's most popular relishes.

The summer of 1853 was spent travelling. He paid young

[1] See Appendix E.

Alexis in Paris a long-promised visit, and acknowledged him as his son. In August, while visiting a 'W. Tucker, Esq., of Corrington Park, Axminster', who was a prominent mason, Soyer was made a 'Sovereign Prince Rose Croix'. It may be a coincidence that the regalia attached to this particular Masonic dignity is among the most beautiful and most elaborate borne by any Mason.

When the Prince Consort visited Napoleon to inspect the camps at Boulogne, Soyer thought it would be an excellent chance to pay a flying visit to his old friend Leon, valet to the emperor. Only pausing to get some magnificent pineapples as a gift for the emperor, he set off without a passport; the customs officers refused to allow him to land, but M. Cossard, a fellow-chef who happened to be on the boat, offered to try to get bail from some of their mutual friends in Boulogne. Soyer was marched off to prison, to await the next boat back to England, while kindly M. Cossard, despite his bulk and the heat of the day, bustled through the town trying to find security for him.

Meanwhile, the parcel of pines, being addressed to the emperor, went straight through the customs, and the fruit was being admired on the imperial table while its donor languished in the lock-up. Eventually, M. Cossard produced some respectable citizens to vouch for Soyer, who thanked them all very heartily, and went off blithely to dine with Leon. Champagne flowed freely at the reunion, and it was three o'clock before Soyer returned to his hotel. For a final smoke, he twisted a piece of paper lying on the table to make a spill, and threw down the last fragment on the floor. At five o'clock he was roused by Cossard, who had mislaid his own passport, and was anxiously enquiring for it everywhere.

'Have I seen it? Of course not, my dear fellow', said Soyer, half-asleep.

'But what is this?' cried Cossard, picking up a scrap of paper from the floor. 'What do I see? "Nez ordinaire!" This is my passport, Soyer, it describes my nose! You come over without a passport, I get you one; you are thrown into prison, I release you; then you burn my own passport, to get me into trouble. It is too bad!'

In vain Soyer protested his innocence, his regret, his condition when he got home, the potency of Leon's champagne; his reputation as a practical joker was remembered against him, and M. Cossard, always believing that the passport had been burned deliberately, never forgave him.

Whatever else he was doing, Soyer still found time for writing. In December 1852 he revised and wrote a new preface for the thirtieth thousand of the *Modern Housewife*, and supervised the production of the eighth edition of the *Gastronomic Regenerator*. He was not content merely to revise old works. He had always wanted to write on the cookery of the ancients, and in 1853 published an enormous tome, *The Pantropheon, or the History of Food and its Preparation from the Earliest Ages of the World*. This volume, produced, as a reviewer remarked, 'in regal style', is a compendium of scraps of information, with a most formidable list of nearly three thousand learned references—'Lampid. In Elogab.', 'Sidon Apollin. Epist. ii. 2', 'Diodor. Sicul.' and so on.

Soyer dealt in detail with every imaginable kind of aliment, tracing its story from the dawn of history. Indeed, the chapter on 'Grinding of Corn' opens with a glance at 'a very distant period, when gods not over-edifying in their conduct descended at times from the heights of Olympus to enliven their immortality amongst mortals' and the book is brought up to date by the inclusion of a description of Soyer's own dinner to Prince Albert at York.

As usual the press was kind. *The Pantropheon* was 'a book of luxurious reading abounding in classic anecdote and olden gossip';[1] it was 'elegant, instructive and interesting, copiously and richly illustrated'.[2] *Punch* enquired what a Pantropheon

[1] *The Illustrated London News*, 10th Sept. 1853.
[2] *United Services Gazette*, 16th Sept. 1853.

might be,[1] and a facetious reviewer suggested that an author who 'discourses so classically on various dainties' wrote 'with a skewer dipped in the dripping-pan of modern Greece'.

In the last edition of the *Modern Housewife* Hortense had promised Eloise to write a cookery book for the 'artisan, mechanic and cottager', and in 1854 it was produced, with the title of *Soyer's Shilling Cookery*. It, too, was written as a correspondence between the two ladies, and though in his usual writing Soyer loved flowery metaphors, chased after all possible puns and delighted in purple patches, in this book he adapted his style to his audience. The receipts are admirably lucid, simple enough for a beginner to follow, varied enough to satisfy an exacting family and economical enough for poor homes.

Successful as his writings had been, this book surpassed them all. Ten thousand copies were sold on the day of publication, sixty thousand went in six weeks, and within a year the hundred and tenth thousand was printed. In 1856 a sixth edition brought the number of copies up to a hundred and forty-five thousand, and forty thousand more were sold in the next three years; sales reached—and passed—a quarter of a million, and in 1867 the publishers produced the two hundred and sixty-fourth thousand.

Though pre-eminently a town and not a country dweller, Soyer was sometimes persuaded to spend a day or two out of London. He became attached to Virginia Water—'the *Paradis Champêtre* of England'—and there he spent much of the summer of 1854. 'This spot', he wrote, 'is little known to the English in general, and to many who have travelled over the world, but as no such delightful place exists anywhere but in England, how can it possibly interest an Englishman? First, it is too close for the wealthy, and too far for the people, being six miles by coach from either Windsor or Staines. The greatest number of visitors I counted daily was about twenty or thirty round the lake, which is seven and a half miles in

<hr>

[1] *Punch*, 29th Oct. 1853.

circumference. I should also observe that Louis Napoleon, being a man of great taste, has imitated it in the Bois de Boulogne as nearly as possible; and by going there every Englishman will have an idea of that which he possesses at home, without troubling himself while in London to go as far as Virginia Water.'

Soyer became popular with the local worthies, and especially with Jennings, the landlord of the 'Wheatsheaf Inn'; together they produced some remarkable dinners. Soyer had not grown out of his love of fooling. Once when his *vis-à-vis* at the end of a long table was Mr Smith of the Theatre Royal, Drury Lane, a waiter appeared after the removes had been taken away, staggering under an immense dish—obviously a saddle of mutton or a sirloin of beef. Mr Smith scolded the man for not bringing in the dish before, but cleared a place for it and sharpened his knife, asking who would have the joint. The cover was lifted—a tiny squirrel jumped out and up on to Mr Smith's shoulder, then raced along from guest to guest. At first Soyer appeared vastly surprised, but presently fell into one of his fits of almost uncontrollable laughter, in which the guests, and even Mr Smith, had to join.

Usually the dishes were edible—supremely edible. Though banished from town, Soyer constantly had parties of friends staying with him, and among them old Lawrence, the farmer who had supplied the whole ox for the dinner at Exeter. Lawrence had retired, and had bought an estate in Yorkshire, where he was reckoned a squire. Soyer had stayed with him, and taught his housekeeper how to make soup for the labourers on the estate, and now Lawrence returned the visit. On the last day a banquet was given in his honour, and at every fresh dish which he tasted the old man cried, 'Well! hang me if I know what stuff I am eating, but it's precious good!' He was helped to bed 'rather top-heavy', and, it is said, fancied himself at home 'blowing up his old woman for having let the cat into the dairy, and being unable to find his gun to shoot her'.

Another guest travelled to London on the same coach the next day, and later told Soyer that the squire was amazed to find himself without a headache, and as hungry as a hunter. He had been certain that after such a feast, such a mixture of strange dishes, such wines, liquors and spirits, he would be ill and unable to eat anything for a couple of days. Quite the contrary—he had eaten a hearty breakfast at Staines, and never felt better. Soyer was not surprised; 'I should have been astonished', he wrote pompously, 'if my dinner had produced the contrary effect; a dinner well-conceived and properly executed, coupled with well-selected beverages, is more than half-digested.'

Parties and picnics were the order of the day. Jennings declared that Soyer was 'the life of the countryside', and Mary the barmaid was never tired of describing the wonders of his 'feet shampeters', as she called them. Soyer loved to preside over a table in the open air, in the long avenue of beech trees facing the water, where the dappled sunlight fell on all kinds of delicate and surprising dishes. After dining the party would wander by the lake, and if it was very fine the ladies would be persuaded to abandon their bonnets and stroll, as one of them ambiguously observed, 'with nothing but their parasols to screen them from the sun'.

These pleasant little affairs served to pass the time, but offered no opportunity for display on the grand scale Soyer loved. He could not live so quietly and obscurely, and made plans to open a restaurant in Paris for the proposed Exhibition there in 1855. A site was chosen; he began to draw up detailed designs. But while he was giving his pleasant beautifully organised picnics at Virginia Water, the British Army was enduring an unpleasant disorganised picnic in the East; next summer, instead of supplying elegant Parisiennes with the most delicate of feasts in a glorified Gore House, Soyer was to be supplying a whole army with the bare necessities of life on the Crimean peninsula.

A CULINARY CAMPAIGN

BY A. SOYER.

ILLUSTRATED BY H. G. HINE.

Title-page of *Soyer's Culinary Campaign*

CHAPTER XII

SOYER AT SCUTARI

'We heard also in that valley a continual howling and yelling, as of a people under unutterable misery, who sat there bound in affliction and irons: and over that valley hang the discouraging clouds of confusion: death also does always spread his wings over it. In a word, it is every whit dreadful, being utterly without order.'

BUNYAN, *The Pilgrim's Progress*

DURING the Crimean war the public, for the first time, received frequent and unbiased accounts of the state of the army in the field; it was the first war 'covered' by professional civilian war correspondents. The most famous of these was Mr Russell of *The Times*, and despite official attempts to check him he sent home tales of mismanagement and ignorance, of departments at cross-purposes, of neglect and stupidity, until it became clear that the terrible mortality among the soldiers was not due to any action of the enemy, but to the muddling and inefficiency of their own officials at home and at the front.[1]

From the beginning of the campaign in May 1854 the record is a pitiful one of error piled upon error, till during the winter of 1854–5 the situation became desperate. The army was encamped on the bare plateau before Sebastopol, without shelter, without fuel, without clothes, without everything. All supplies had to come from the tiny port of Balaclava, seven miles away, over a track which was a sea of mud seamed with deep crevasses, completely impassable for wheeled traffic. The men were without cooking equipment, and did not know how to cook had they had it. They lived on biscuit and rum and salt pork, when they got them, but often it was impossible to find fuel to cook the meat, and some regiments threw away

[1] A fuller account, *Chaos in the Crimea*, by the author will be found in the *Army Quarterly*, 1939.

a hundred pounds of it every day. The commissary-general was an octogenarian civilian, responsible to the Treasury for every penny he spent, and desperately afraid of doing anything without signed permission from England.

The base hospitals were at Scutari, great bare Turkish barracks built over pestilential sewers, without even enough beds to keep the wounded off the floors, short of shirts, pillows, blankets, knives and forks, pails, baths, towels, soap, and the most essential medicines. Over them ruled Treasury officials, whose only idea was to spend as little as possible as slowly as possible, and who were far more concerned to save money than to save men.

When Russell and other civilians wrote home accounts of the horrors they had seen, all was denied; the public were assured that the accusations were baseless, and the medical officers concealed the truth even from each other. The authorities could and did forbid strangers to enter the wards, but they could not silence the men who survived, they could not prevent Miss Nightingale from disclosing what she saw, and soon all England rang with the scandal. Through all the darkness of confused stories and contradictory reports, the public saw one figure clearly enough—a Lady with a Lamp. It is a pity that its rays did not extend a little farther, to disclose her constant helper and associate—a Man with a Patent Stove.

On 16th January 1855 a letter from a soldier at the front appeared in *The Times*, begging M. Soyer to advise the men how to use their rations. On 22nd January his reply appeared, a few receipts entitled 'simplified cookery for the army'. When his attention had thus been caught, Soyer started to read Russell's dispatches every day, with ever-increasing interest and horror.

On 2nd February he attended the pantomime at Drury Lane, and went on for supper to his favourite eating-house, the 'Albion'. Waiting for his friends, he read the latest news from the war, and here, the scene of Sheriffs' breakfasts, corporation functions, East India Company banquets, smoking concerts, and all the comfortable festivities in which he delighted, Soyer on the spur of the moment made the decision which was to involve him in immense labour, acute discomfort and severe illness, and to give him a lasting importance in the history of the British Army.

He wrote to *The Times*:

Sir—After carefully perusing the letter of your correspondent, dated Scutari, in your impression of Wednesday last, I perceive that, although the kitchen under the superintendence of Miss Nightingale affords so much relief, the system of management at the large one in the Barrack Hospital is far from being perfect. I propose offering my services gratuitously, and proceeding direct to Scutari, at my own personal expense, to regulate that important department, if the Government will honour me with their confidence, and grant me the full power of acting according to my knowledge and experience in such matters.

> I have the honour to remain, Sir,
>
> Your obedient servant, A. SOYER.

The press revelations about the condition of the army, and the ratting of Lord John Russell at a critical moment, had caused the fall of the Aberdeen ministry at the end of January, and Lord Panmure had replaced Newcastle and Herbert at the War Office. Panmure was anxious to do everything possible to placate public opinion, and not only jumped at Soyer's offer to go to Scutari, but asked him to visit the Crimea also, and to do what he could to reform the methods of army cooking generally. At their interview Soyer criticised the standard camp kettles, which were absurdly small, a twelve-pint kettle being issued to every eight men. Perhaps Panmure remembered that the dreaded *Times* correspondent had described the stoves in use as 'wretched affairs...made of thin sheet iron which cannot stand our fuel, charcoal...mere poison manufactures',[1] for Soyer was asked to design a new stove.

At once he began to experiment, not only contriving new dishes from the standard rations, but inventing a kind of ground baked peas-meal which on the addition of boiling

[1] Three officers died on 4th December 1854 from using them in their tents.

water became a thick comforting soup, quickly made in an emergency. He designed a portable cooking stove, equally suitable for use in camp or in the hospitals, which would consume a minimum of fuel, and in a few days he triumphantly carried a model of it to the War Office. Lord Panmure and the Duke of Cambridge were enthusiastic, and Brunel (the great engineer) decided to use it at the base hospitals at Smyrna and Rankioi.

This stove was Soyer's most notable invention; it was eventually adopted for use by the entire army, and is still, as General MacMunn wrote in 1935, 'among the most essential articles of camp equipment'. Nowadays a petrol pressure lamp is sometimes used in place of other fuels, but the stove is fundamentally the same as when Soyer designed it. The inventor refused to patent it, lest people should think his offer had been made only for his own profit, but, as always, found it easier to let the cash go than the credit, and had his name and label put on every stove.

Receipts and stoves, it seemed, could be produced easily enough, but assistants to carry out the receipts and demonstrate the stoves were another matter. Everyone was terrified of Crimean fever; Russell had done his work so well that it was thought that to go to the East was to go to almost certain death. Sala refused to accompany Soyer as secretary, and the man who was engaged in his stead was persuaded at the last moment, by anxious relations, to stay at home. Driving along Piccadilly on his last morning, Soyer happened to meet a friend whom he describes as 'T. G., a gentleman of colour', and somehow persuaded him to join the party as secretary, leaving that very evening. They were sent off at the station with three cheers, 'the echo of which', says Soyer, 'still vibrates in my heart, and was through the whole of my culinary campaign a high source of gratification to my feelings.'[1]

[1] Soyer's own descriptions of his Crimean venture are taken from his book *Soyer's Culinary Campaign*, which he published on his return.

Still one more misadventure delayed them next morning at Folkestone—the disappearance of the pocket-book which contained most of their introductions and valuables. T. G. was sent back to London in case it had been lost there, and the town-crier announced its loss in the streets of Folkestone; there was a tremendous to-do, until at last it was found stuck in the frame of Soyer's bed. 'Upon this discovery', he says, 'I immediately telegraphed for T. G. to return, in these words, "Stop a gentleman of colour—it's all right." On the arrival of the train at Tonbridge, the cry of "Stop the gentleman of colour" was loudly shouted along the station. "All right, all right", cried T. G.; "Here I am." He immediately jumped into the down train, and arrived time enough to save [*sic*] the steamer.'

One day was spent making a tour of the military hospitals in Paris, and taking note of their kitchen arrangements and diets. During part of the journey through France, they travelled with a party of lady volunteers bound for Smyrna as nurses; the ladies were astounded by Soyer and his followers, but the Lady Superintendent accepted a signed copy of one of the *chef*'s books. One of the nurses was pleased enough when Soyer patted her shoulder, till a giggling friend asked if that was a 'pâté de foie gras'; she was then offended, but it was just the joke to please Soyer.

At Marseilles he had hoped to find suitable provision merchants to supply the army, but was disappointed. 'With such a stock of provisions', he wrote, 'any Government might keep its army in a state of perfect *starvation* . . . though at the same time the quantity and quality might have served very well for a dainty picnic of a couple of thousand epicures, the price being so high.'

Before embarking they dined at the 'Reserve' on the famed Marseilles *Bouillabaisse*, that 'rich and savoury stew' which, Thackery wrote,

a noble dish is,
A sort of soup or broth or brew
Or hotch-potch of all sorts of fishes,
That Greenwich never could outdo.

Greenwich might be outdone, but not Soyer. The host, on learning who he was, gave him the receipt, and he instantly composed a *Bouillabaisse à l'Anglaise*, which, he claimed, possessed 'two great qualities; first, to suit the palate of the gourmet; second, being very strengthening'.

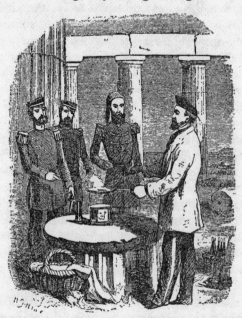

Soyer in the Parthenon

The voyage was rough but otherwise uneventful. A visit to Ajaccio produced a letter to the press, headed 'Twenty Minutes in the Kitchen of the House of the Emperor Napoleon the First', and *The Illustrated London News* received from Athens a description of a *déjeuner à la fourchette* cooked on the Magic Stove 'in the ancient Parthenon...on a fallen capital of the stupendous ruins'.

The skyline of Constantinople was as famous then as that of New York to-day, and Soyer sailed up the Bosphorus on a beautiful clear morning—luckier than Miss Nightingale, who had landed in a deluge of rain that made Constantinople 'look like a bad Daguerreotype washed out'. When the enormous Barrack Hospital was pointed out Soyer realised fully, for the first time, the immensity of the task he had undertaken, and his spirits momentarily sank. Thousands of patients lay there, each requiring three or four meals daily; the kitchens were unequipped and inconveniently placed; the cooks were unskilled and the arrangements for supply chaotic; he knew nothing of his colleagues, who were likely to resent the introduction of a stranger, especially a civilian, to teach them their business, and the country was completely strange to him.

His spirits rose as he saw Constantinople itself spread before him. From the ship it appeared enchantingly lovely, a mass of domes and cupolas and minarets piled up by some Arabian sorcerer. Disillusionment was swift; at the landing-place the first thing to strike the eye—and nose—were the heaps of manure which lay around, and the carcass of a dead horse, which swung on the surface of the water, while pariah dogs flung themselves upon it and retired snarling as it floated out of reach. The traveller had to pick his way to his hotel through dark and narrow streets, full of black and liquid mud.

To realise the magnitude of the problem with which Soyer had to grapple, it is necessary to outline the system by which patients in military hospitals were fed. A man was placed on full, half, low or spoon diet. The daily allowance for full diet was one pound of meat, one pound of bread, one pound of potatoes, two pints of tea and half a pint of porter. Half diet was exactly half of this, and low diet half again of that, while spoon diet was simply one pound of bread and two pints of tea. Extras might only be given to men on spoon diet. The diet rolls were written by sergeants or corporals appointed as ward masters, and before these rolls could be sent to the purveyor's office they had to be signed by the assistant surgeon and countersigned by the staff surgeon. In the over-crowded and understaffed wards at Scutari this system led to endless confusion and delay. The surgeons had no time to sign and countersign requisitions, and before Soyer's arrival the men who could not manage to swallow the ordinary food often went hungry.

The only apparatus for cooking left by the Turks when they vacated the Barrack Hospital consisted of thirteen large copper boilers in a kitchen at the end of the yard. Only eight of these were usable. During the winter of 1854–5 these eight coppers, with a few tin pots on open braziers, had to supply three to four miles of beds, that is, 1900 to 2500 patients, with three meals daily. Not only were utensils lacking, but the system of management was almost incredibly inefficient. The meat was issued to the ward orderlies by a single man from one office, nominally from nine to twelve-thirty. Many of the orderlies did not in fact get their joints and take them to the kitchens till half-past one. They had, as Soyer afterwards noted, 'a most curious method of marking their different lots. Some used a piece of red cloth cut from an old jacket; others half-a-dozen buttons tied together; old knives, forks, scissors, etc., but one in particular had hit upon the idea...of tying a pair of old snuffers to the lot. All this rubbish was daily boiled with the meat, and probably required more cooking. On telling the man that it was a very dirty trick to put such things in the soup, his reply was "How can it be dirty, sir? Sure, they have been boiling this last month."'

The orderlies were supposed to receive the cooked meat at one o'clock, but as those who had put their meat in first were not necessarily the first to get it out, some of the meat was boiled to rags, some left almost raw. Each orderly took his bundle of joints to his own bed, where he divided the meat into portions and distributed the rations to his patients, who might not be fed till half-past three or even later. When the food did come, it was often enough uneatable. 'The waste in the wards', said Miss Nightingale, 'was enormous, because the men were really unable to eat diets so badly cooked'; Miss Taylor, one of the lady volunteers, agreed that 'after a man had been put on half or even full diet the surgeons were often obliged to return him to spoon diet from his not being able to eat the meat.'

So much for the ordinary diets. Before Miss Nightingale's arrival in November 1854 there were no arrangements at all for supplying extra-diets. She at once set aside a room in the Barrack Hospital as an extra-diet kitchen (where she used the Duke of Cambridge's *batterie de cuisine*, which he had left her when he returned home) and a second room was fitted out about Christmas 1854. Three boilers for hot water were set up on a staircase, and occasionally one of the boilers in the main kitchen was used for arrowroot or fowls. Sometimes the orderlies cooked for the patients in their own mess tins and at first the lady volunteers also tried to cook in the wards on their private 'Etnas'. They persuaded a few surgeons to write requisitions for dry stores, and made lemonade and beef tea for the men, but soon this was stopped by an order from Dr Cumming, the inspector-general, that no cooking was to be done in the wards. Miss Taylor, one of the lady volunteers, observed bitterly that 'amid all the confusion and distress of Scutari Hospital, military discipline was never lost sight of, and an infringement of one of its smallest observances was worse than letting twenty men die of neglect'. 'The poor men', wrote S. G. O.[1] in *The Times*, 'were in the matter of their meals shamefully dealt with.'

All this time Dr Menzies was telling the ambassador that nothing was wanted. Afterwards, when questioned by the Roebuck Committee about the scarcity of food, he said that 'he did not *think* any deaths occurred from this cause'; Mr Bracebridge,[2] however, wrote to Herbert that 'no doubt

[1] The Rev. Lord Sidney Godolphin Osborne, whose revelations of the hospital conditions did much to bring about reform.

[2] Mr Bracebridge and his wife were personal friends of Miss Nightingale, who had come out with her to Scutari.

many have been lost from want of nourishment, not being able to eat the food they get.' S. G. O. praised Miss Nightingale for her extra-diet kitchens, and the 'timely messes of well-cooked, nourishing, wholesome food' which her orderlies distributed, but she herself knew how little could be done without reconstruction of the whole system. At the beginning of February she found that her kitchens could feed seven hundred of the worst cases, though without proper cooks it was a continual struggle. 'This is not so amusing', she told Herbert, 'as pottering and messing about with little cookeries of individual beef tea for the poor sufferers personally, and my ladies do not like it.' She was not allowed to make any general reforms. It would have been a great improvement to have had the meat issued from the stores boned, so that each patient would get some meat, instead of sometimes finding his portion all bone or all gristle, but the inspector-general informed her that it would require 'a new Regulation of the Service' to bone the meat.

In the General Hospital conditions were, if anything, worse. Only five of the eleven coppers could be used, and in the kitchen the brickwork was loose; as the fuel was supplied from inside the building, the kitchen was always full of smoke.

Now came Soyer, with Lord Panmure's authority to have the meat issued as he pleased. Miss Nightingale had heard before of his philanthropic activities, for in December 1846 her Aunt Ju (Mrs Julia Smith) had attended Soyer's classes to teach ladies how to make cheap soup for the 'hungry poors'. All the lady volunteers welcomed him. 'His good-natured and cheerful countenance', wrote Lady Alicia Blackwood, 'was quite refreshing, and his presence was hailed with much welcome as a very useful adjunct to a very needful department. His peculiar appearance also enlivened the monotony of our everyday routine. M. Soyer's dress corresponded with the bent of his mind, which was in all things devoted to his profession; he clothed himself completely in white, excepting only his cap, which was large and wide and made of dark-blue cloth edged with a gold binding.... His thoughts seemed concentrated on his own hobby, it was paramount, the beginning, continuation, and ending of everything with him. Even his plan for taking Sebastopol was to be entirely by starvation; he could see no reason why lives were to be sacrificed by gunpowder when the *cuisine* failure would do it all. In any case the arrival of M. Soyer was a cheering and cheerful addition, for we all, more or less, benefited by his coming, and we thankfully record it when we revert to those times.'

Miss Nightingale herself showed Soyer round the Barrack Hospital. Her own extra-diet kitchens, though cramped and ill-equipped, were clean and orderly, but the kitchens run by the soldiers were 'in the greatest confusion...full of smoke, and everything was boiling too fast...everything had the disagreeable flavour of being burnt'. Miss Nightingale recorded that 'Soyer was almost as shocked by the state of the great coppers where the cooking was done as the Sanitary Commissioners had been by the state of the latrines'.

At the General Hospital, Miss Nightingale had been refused permission to start an extra-diet kitchen, but a Dr O'Flaherty had later managed to organise one, which was comparatively well run. Soyer remarks that Dr O'Flaherty had seen the model soup-kitchen in Dublin in 1847, and leaves the reader to draw his own conclusions.

Shocking as the kitchen premises and utensils were, the methods of the cooks were still more horrifying. 'Such a noise', wrote Soyer, 'I never heard before,...the market at old Billingsgate, during the first morning sale, was nothing compared to this military row. Each man had two tin cans for the soup. They kept running about and knocking into each other, in most admirable disorder. Such confusion, thought I, is enough to kill a dozen patients daily.' Perhaps his mind flew back to the Reform Club, where, as his secretary had written, 'the minute-hand did not pass more regularly over the face of the clock than the assistants of Soyer revolved round him as the centre planet of their system.'

Money was to be had only grudgingly, and after long delays, but many reforms could be made at once by the expenditure of a little common sense. The joints of meat were tied in bunches to huge wooden skewers before being plunged into the coppers, and the orderlies had always lashed them so tightly together that only the outer end of each joint was cooked. So simple a change as tying them loosely vastly improved the patients' meals. The orderlies had also been in the habit of throwing away the water in which the fresh meat had been boiled. The scandalised Soyer showed them that this water was in fact excellent broth, and the clear white fat which he recovered from the top of it was much preferred by the patients to the expensive—and rancid—butter from the bazaar. The men had only one plate,[1] or rather tin bowl, each, and the orderlies first distributed the meat, and then when it was eaten poured out the soup. Soyer pointed out that if they would pour the soup over the meat, the soup could be drunk first and the meat would meanwhile be kept hot.

He concocted some soup so different from the usual thin and flavourless liquid that the doctors would not believe that it was made from the ordinary rations, and, heartened by this success, he decided that he would the next day cook the soup for the entire hospital. Arriving at the kitchen at seven, he found it bare, and was told that no rations were issued until ten o'clock. At once Soyer bearded the purveyor in his office, and soon, he says, 'my new regiment began to manœuvre

---

[1] Even this was a great improvement on the early days, when the sisters who fed one ward had only one small green pail between them, which was used in turn for beef tea, negus, arrowroot and water. Upon one occasion, only three small spoons could be found for fifty men, whose diet was arrowroot. The orderly officer, when appealed to, simply said, "Every soldier has a spoon, knife and fork, comb, razor, etc., in his knapsack." The sisters asked where they could find the knapsacks, and he replied, "I have not charge of them." They were in fact on the field of the Alma.

admirably under my command'. The resulting soup was the first palatable meal that many of the patients had eaten since first entering the hospital.

Soyer insisted that salt and pepper should be supplied to the cooks so that they could season the food while cooking it, and this was done, though Dr Hall's[1] demands for condiments had been made in vain for months. In a few days the coppers had been retinned, and a charcoal stove and oven built. A storeroom and larder were partitioned off, and fitted with chopping-blocks and dressers. The oddments which had been used to mark the meat were replaced by numbered skewers.

One of the principal causes of the atrocious cooking had been the system whereby the men cooked in rotation. This meant that no sooner had a man grasped the first principles of cooking than his time was up; he returned to his regiment and was replaced by a complete novice. Miss Nightingale had written to Herbert begging for cooks that were *cooks*, and not merely drunken soldiers. Soyer appointed a sergeant as a permanent overseer; detailed instructions and receipts were clearly copied out and hung in the kitchens. The boilers had not been used systematically, each of them might one day be used to cook seventy rations and the next day a hundred and fifty; now each was used for a hundred and fifty rations, and only one had a varying quantity daily according to the total number required. Leaving nothing to chance, Soyer drew up for this boiler a detailed scheme for from five to a hundred diets.

Tea which has been brewed in a copper just emptied of soup is not tea at its best. If it has been made by flinging into hot water some tea tied tightly in a rag, so that only the tea on the outside of the bundle infuses at all, still less is the result a nice cup of tea. Some better method had to be contrived, so Soyer invented his 'Scutari teapot', which in its simpest form was a large kettle, in which was placed a coffee filter to hold the tea. (A modification sold later in England worked on the

[1] Chief medical officer in the Crimea.

same principle, but the lid was a minaret bearing a crescent.)
This was one of Soyer's most popular innovations, but he himself, busy with a hundred
larger matters, regarded it
merely as a *jeu d'esprit*—
'more a happy thought than
an invention'.

When the preparations for
reform at the Barrack and
General Hospitals were
well under way, Lady Stratford de Redcliffe took Soyer
out to inspect the three
smaller hospitals at Koulali,
her own special preserve,
which were then under the
guidance of Miss Stanley.
Miss Stanley had brought
out a second detachment of
nurses and lady volunteers,
meaning to hand them over
to Miss Nightingale; but

Scutari tea-pot

the latter regarded this as a breach of Herbert's promise to
send no more women without her consent, and refused to take
charge of them. (Miss Stanley had made no arrangements to
finance her group, expecting Miss Nightingale to do this.)
One of the women was appointed supervisor at the General
Hospital, the others after some delay went to Koulali.

Miss Nightingale had asked Mrs Herbert to write of her
to Lady Stratford as 'not a lady, but a real hospital nurse, who
has had experience'. Miss Stanley, however, as one of her
nurses said, 'always behaved like a lady—like a real lady',
and she and Lady Stratford became great friends. Miss
Stanley soon gave up 'all but the general direction', and so
had time for tea-parties with Lady Stratford and the wives of

various officers, who enjoyed sailing out to Koulali for a picnic. When she arrived, Miss Stanley 'asked to have a house found, in which it would be possible to receive both visitors and nurses'; at that time 'there was not a Turkish house which was not in a fragmentary state, roof and windows pervious in all directions, not a room in one's quarters which does not let in the rain in showers whenever the weather is bad', and Miss Nightingale herself was sleeping behind a screen in the room used as an extra-diet kitchen.

When on 29th January 1855 Miss Stanley took charge at Koulali, she was greatly relieved to find that there was then 'nothing whatever disagreeable' in the wards. The poor lady had earlier received a severe shock when, as she told Mrs Bracebridge, Sister A—— had said to Sister M——, 'Now then for a hunt!' and begun 'diligently to capture the little lively inhabitants of her dress. "But what do you think?"' Miss Stanley went on, 'Can you imagine? Sister M—— actually found *something* on her gown, actually *something*!' Mrs Bracebridge was not astonished; she was used to the replacement of 'the usual English salutation that the day was fine or wet, hot or cold', by 'the far more sensational and important question of "How many fleas have you caught to-day?"'

Soyer found the main kitchen in the Barrack Hospital at Koulali 'in perfect darkness, full of smoke, blinding the men', who 'even preferred their dangerous duty in the trenches to this kind of culinary inquisition'. (There had just been a fire, as the flue of a chimney was so badly built that if it was heated it burst into flames.) The cooks and orderlies protested so strongly that they were changed every week, or even oftener, and a continual stream of novices cooked shockingly. There was enormous waste of fuel; 'the men actually piled small trees upon the fires, and when the soup boiled too fast they threw pailfuls of water upon the burning wood, filling the place with dust and steam.' The only eatable food served here was that prepared by the Sisters of Mercy in their tiny extra-diet kitchen—their rice pudding is especially praised in many accounts.

At the Convalescent Hospital Soyer found 'neither kitchen nor cooking utensils'. Miss Taylor wrote that 'an ounce of arrowroot or sugar was worth more than its weight in gold, while a saucepan to boil it in, or a spoon to stir it with, was guarded by its fortunate possessor with a dragon-like vigilance'. She describes the arrangements—or lack of them—in some detail. The ordinary diets were cooked in boilers under an open shed, and at first the extra-diets had to be prepared on a few open braziers. Later two of the boilers were used, one for fowls and one for arrowroot. The orderlies stirred up their arrowroot with cold water, in wooden buckets, using bits of stick; the cook then shared out the boiling water, while the orderlies fought to be served first, since there never was enough to go round. The lady in charge put in the wine, and the orderlies carried the resulting brew into the wards.

Soyer soon sketched out plans for improvement, and made lists of requisitions on the purveyor-in-chief. He promised to send them his receipts, with a civilian cook to instruct the men, but had to hurry back to Scutari himself, to open the new kitchens there.

By now his kiosque near the hospital, 'Soyer House', was ready, and he was spared the daily double journey over the Bosphorous. As soon as he had landed at Constantinople he had developed diarrhœa, and this persisted for weeks. It was not lessened by a brief attack of fever, but he was determined not to postpone the grand opening of his improved kitchens, to which all the eminent medical men, and many army officers, English, French and Turkish, had been invited.

On the appointed day Soyer was in his element. He had discarded his uniform white, and was clad in a loose white coat falling open over a gold-braided waistcoat, and trousers with a broad blue and silver stripe, with a turban-like cap of

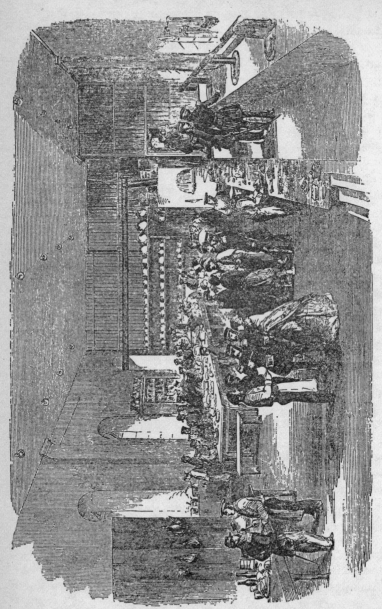

Kitchen at Scutari (from *The Illustrated London News*)

white and red. Moving from one visitor to another, he
watched them taste from numbered bowls the diets as served
before and after his advent, and heard on every side compliments and exclamations of wonder and admiration, not
only about the actual food, but also about the improved
cleanliness and orderliness of the kitchen.[1] His only regret
was that stormy weather prevented Lady Stratford and some
of the Frenchmen and Turks from crossing the Bosphorus,
but their visit was merely postponed; they came instead a few
days later, and he had all the compliments over again.

In England, Soyer had an excellent press; even the sceptical
Mr Punch declared that 'Too many cooks had spoiled the
broth at Scutari, and now M. Soyer has put it all to
rights.'

The day after the opening Soyer cooked for a quarter of the
patients, and three days later took charge of half of them.
After a few more days he transferred his care to the other
half, letting the first patients go back to the old régime. The
immediate outburst of complaints was further proof of the
transformation that had taken place. The soldiers so appreciated Soyer's efforts, said Lady Alicia Blackwood, that 'when
he was passing through the corridors of the Great Barracks one
day he was saluted with a vociferous shout of "Three times
three" from them, cheering with all their strength.' Soon all the
extra-diet kitchens were closed, and the extras were prepared
in the large kitchen. Two civilian cooks, with six soldiers
under them, produced better broth—and everything else—
than their thirty-four untrained and erratic predecessors.

The General Hospital was not neglected. Soyer used to
ride from one hospital to another on a small pony, supervising
the cooks, planning new ovens and dressers, showing one

[1] Lord William Paulet wrote down on the spot his opinion that 'Had
I not seen and tasted them [the new diets] I could not have believed
that such an amelioration could have been produced from the same
materials as allowed by Government. . . . I could not have believed that
difference could have been produced by rearrangement and a really
simple art of cooking, and a proper organisation of proportions.'

man how to season beef tea, and another how to construct a chimney. Soon the patients in the General Hospital were as well served as those in the Barrack Hospital.

In the middle of the latter Soyer had a special shed of his own, and on the table there 'was always an ample display of everything good and useful in the way of nourishment—from plain rice-water to jellies and strong soups. The dishes were all made from the articles distributed as rations, and he was ever ready to instruct those that were willing to learn how to convert them to palatable food.'

It was now the middle of April. All these changes had happened in less than a month.

Miss Stanley had gone home, and her successor at Koulali, Miss Hutton, asked Soyer to revisit the hospitals there. 'A few days of your instruction and superintendence', she wrote, 'might effect more good than I can express.' Largely owing to her own energy and ability, all the improvements which had been planned during his first visit had been carried out, and little remained to be done, except at the Convalescent Hospital. The so-called kitchen there belonged to the Turkish authorities, and could not be altered without an order from them. It was decided that, even though it was 'a difficult matter to get a plank, or even a nail, fixed in any of the hospitals', it would be quicker to build a new kitchen than to apply to the Turkish authorities; the building was at once begun.

The lady volunteers had always considered the tea issued from the general kitchen 'the most wretched stuff possible', and one of them writes that when Soyer demonstrated his new teapot at Koulali it was 'much better, and yet he made it with the same proportions as before'. She goes on, 'M. Soyer made his tea in a little kitchen outside the Convalescent Hospital. The medical officers and ladies came to taste it, and it was an amusing scene; the group outside tasting the tea, the tiny kitchen which just held M. Soyer and his assistants, and the patients in the Convalescent Hospital looking and wondering what was to happen to their tea that night.'

The Scutari hospitals were now so organised that Soyer's personal supervision was not necessary, and he made up his mind to go up to the Crimea. He had only to wait until an efficient purveyor could be sent from England to take charge of the issuing of stores, and soon a Mr Robertson arrived. Although it was rumoured that he was 'a very old and infirm man, wearing green spectacles', Mr Robertson proved to be in fact a complete contrast to his aged predecessor, the Peninsula veteran, Mr Wreford. The new purveyor was only thirty years old, vigorous, intelligent, and best of all, willing and even eager to purvey. A revolution took place in the department. Anything in store or obtainable in local markets was supplied on demand. The men were actually given fruit.

Mr Robertson was all that could be desired, but in order to keep the diets up to their new standard, the doctors were asked to send unexpectedly now and then for a bowl of soup. When Soyer asked Lord William Paulet to do this too, he was delighted to find that it was his lordship's regular habit to lunch off 'a bowl of the soldiers' soup'. Lord William was wise; private cooking was such that one cook—whose master had previously been envied—was found emptying the dregs of oil from the corridor lamps into his pan to fry fish for a dinner-party.

The patent stoves had not arrived, but Soyer would not wait, especially as Miss Nightingale and Mr Bracebridge were also going up to the Crimea. On 2nd May 1855, accompanied by the faithful T. G. and four soldier cooks, he embarked on the 'Robert Lowe' for the front.

CHAPTER XIII

CULINARY CAMPAIGN: VENI

'No soldier can fight unless he is properly fed on beer and beef.'
Attributed to the DUKE OF MARLBOROUGH

As they sailed down the Bosphorus on a perfect May morning they heard guns crashing out a salute to the Sultan as he went in procession to the Mosque of Sultan Mahomet. Soyer was enraptured by the loveliness of the weather and the beauty of the shores—'What a glorious mine of subjects for a Claude Lorraine, mademoiselle!' he said to Miss Nightingale. 'It is much to be regretted that he never visited these Moslem shores.' They were passing the Koulali hospitals, and Miss Nightingale characteristically answered his praise of their situation by criticism of their sanitation, and enquiries about the schemes for its improvement. The voyage should have been a time of rest and recuperation, but neither Miss Nightingale nor Soyer could rest if there was work to be done. They drew up plans for their work at the front, Miss Nightingale spent much time ministering to some invalids on board, and Soyer quickly found his way to the galley, where he not only investigated and improved the cooking arrangements, but began to make notes for a work on naval cookery in general.

Each recognised and respected the other's singlemindedness, and Soyer expressed his admiration in an account of Miss Nightingale written about this time. 'She is rather high in stature, fair in complexion, and slim in person; her hair is brown, and is worn quite plain; her physiognomy is most pleasing; her eyes, of a bluish tint, speak volumes, and are always sparkling with intelligence; her mouth is small and well-formed, while her lips act in unison, and make known the impression of her heart—one seems the reflex of the other. Her visage, as regards expression, is very remarkable, and one can almost anticipate by her countenance what she is about to say: alternatively, with matters of the most grave import, a gentle smile passes radiantly over her countenance, thus proving the evenness of her temper; at other times, when wit or a pleasantry prevails, the heroine is lost in the happy, good-natured smile which pervades her face, and you recognise only the charming woman. Her dress is generally of a greyish or black tint; she wears a simple white cap, and often a rough apron. In a word, her whole appearance is religiously simple and unsophisticated. In conversation no member of the fair sex can be more amiable and gentle than Miss Nightingale. Removed from her arduous and cavalier-like duties, which require the nerve of a Hercules—and she posesses it when required—she is Rachel on the stage in both tragedy and comedy.'

The company was enlivened by the addition of one Peter Morrison—always referred to as P. M.—who had attached himself to Soyer at Scutari. He was courting a wealthy lady, who had refused to consider the advances of any man who had not 'both fought and bled for his country', so P. M. had seized the chance of going to the front as Soyer's secretary. Unfortunately, as they approached the enemy his courage 'oozed out at his fingers' ends' and Soyer rather unkindly remarks that P. M. preferred 'the shelter of the bays in my kitchen to any laurels he might reap on the field of Mars'. A looking-glass on board had been broken in a storm by a steward's head, and on being told in jest that it had been 'shattered by a round-shot' P. M. became most alarmed. 'Well,' he said, 'I do not like the job I have undertaken. You don't mean to say our lives will be endangered at Balaclava?'—'Oh dear no, not in the least, unless they fire on us!'—'I tell you what,' cried P. M., 'I will not stand it, for I bargained for nothing of the kind!'

His fears increased as they entered the harbour of Balaclava and saw the words 'Cossack Bay' painted on a rock, which two or three Turks were approaching. P. M. asked if they were enemies, and Soyer replied that he thought they were. 'I say Monsieur Soyer,' exclaimed P. M., 'this is beyond a joke, for if those ugly fellows choose to fire upon us, they can do so as easily as possible.' 'No doubt they can', said Soyer. '*I* shall not give them a chance!' called P. M. over his shoulder as he fled below. His trials had hardly begun. A terrible cannonade was heard in the evening, and P. M. thought that all chance of escape was gone; he must have expressed the feelings of many of the combatants when he exclaimed, 'Oh, give me London and Red Lion Square before any of your seats of war, for I see no fun in glory!'

There was not a house, a hut, or even a tent to be had in Balaclava, and during this visit the whole party lived aboard various ships in the harbour, moving from one to the other as the transports came and went. They landed every day, and toiled through the mud to the various hospitals, over roads of 'a slippery sticky sort of wet clay, which sends you sliding as though you walked on ice'. There was enough to be done to satisfy the most eager worker; the buildings were primitive; the kitchens were almost non-existent.

In January 1855 the 'kitchen' of the General Hospital at Balaclava (which was by far the best equipped of any hospital in the Crimea) had contained only three coppers, two of which were used for soup and the other for extra-diets. By May an oven had been built in the main kitchen and a separate hut (part of which had been used previously as a Protestant chapel) allotted to preparations for extra-diets. This was put in charge of one of the nurses, Mrs Elizabeth Davis, who had given the authorities at Scutari no peace until she was sent to the Crimea itself. She resented Miss Nightingale's authority from the first—'I did not like the name of Nightingale. When I first hear a name I am very apt to know by my feelings whether I shall like the person that bears it'—and her stories of her encounters with Miss Nightingale cannot always be believed. Her accounts of conditions at Balaclava, however, are borne out by other evidence, and there is no doubt at all of her immense courage and energy. She worked from 5 a.m. till midnight almost every day, not only cooking breakfast, dinner, tea and supper, but dealing out arrowroot and wine at all hours to the orderlies, and even finding time to feed the patients who were too weak to lift their fingers to their mouths.

For a time she had 'a quiet useful man' to help her, as orderly, but he fell sick, and his successors were either 'idle tipsy fellows' or, if sober, unbearably stupid. One was so ignorant that when given a fowl to prepare he skinned it. She decided that she could work better alone than with such assistants, and somehow she got the work done. The miserable hut used as an extra-diet kitchen was also her bedroom. 'I had often by day', she wrote, 'to select a spot where I might find shelter from the rain, while giving out the rations. At night I have frequently had to lay [sic] soaking with the rain pouring down on me.'

The cooking for the men on full diet and for the hospital orderlies was done in the main kitchen by an old Scottish pensioner, Peter Frank, and he allowed Mrs Davis to bake a few things in his oven, but everything else she had to cook on braziers. Lady Stratford had sent up a stove with two ovens, but some of the flues and fittings were lost on the way, and the useless ovens lay about for a time, until someone carried them off. Soyer, who had found that most of the soldier-cooks knew nothing at all of cooking, and were unwilling to learn, was amazed and delighted to find Frank eager to be taught the new methods. The independent Mrs Davis was less amenable, regarding Soyer suspiciously as a colleague of Miss Nightingale, but he praised her for doing so much without utensils or stoves, and pleased her by promising to have her kitchen rebuilt and properly equipped.

At the Sanatorium, on the Genoese Heights, the meals were prepared in kitchens 'built of mud, exposed to the open air, unroofed, and burning much fuel', and in 'mud mounts called cook-houses'; Soyer decided to replace them by a simple and infinitely more convenient central kitchen.

On the second day it was decided to ride over to the camp to see Lord Raglan. He had called on Miss Nightingale the day before, but she had been out inspecting the hospitals, and had not seen him. So crowded were the streets of the port that the little party of nine took half-an-hour to cover the first mile of the journey. The road was narrow, the surface execrable, and it was packed with Greeks, Armenians, Jews and Maltese; with mules, horses, donkeys; with artillery wagons, ration parties, pack animals, cannons; and with infantry and cavalry, French, Turkish and English. The extraordinary sight of an English lady—Miss Nightingale was 'attired simply in a genteel amazone, or riding-habit, and had quite a martial air'—caused such crowds to collect that traffic was brought to a standstill. The horses became restive, prancing and kicking, and the wretched P. M.'s mule—known as 'Clockwork' because when once wound up there was no stopping it—almost unseated him again and again by its violent plunging.

They were disappointed to find neither Lord Raglan nor Dr Hall (the chief medical officer) at home, but nevertheless went on to the General Hospital before Sebastopol, where Soyer shook his head over the 'gipsy cooking encampment' where all the meals had to be prepared, while Miss Nightingale went round the wards. News of her visit caused great excitement among the men, and she was sent off with three cheers and then three times three.

Wishing to have a closer view of Sebastopol, they rode up to the head of the Woronzoff Road. P. M. followed them doubtfully, reassuring himself by remarking, 'I say, Monsieur Soyer, of course you would not take Miss Nightingale where there will be any danger?' Someone proposed going nearer still, and though the sentry tried to dissuade them, Miss Nightingale insisted on going on. P. M. was horrified—'I say, where the deuce are you all going?'—and when a shell came whistling overhead he was convinced that it had been aimed at him, and flung himself down behind Soyer for shelter.

When they reached Three-Mortar Battery, and saw Sebastopol spread clearly before them, Soyer succumbed to his love for dramatic gestures. 'Before leaving the battery,' he writes, 'I begged Miss Nightingale, as a favour, to give me her hand, which she did. I then requested her to ascend the stone rampart next the wooden gun-carriage, and lastly, to sit upon the centre mortar, to which she very gracefully and kindly acceded. I then boldly exclaimed, "Gentlemen, behold this amiable lady sitting fearlessly upon that terrible instrument of war! Behold the heroic daughter of England— the soldier's friend!" All present shouted "Bravo! bravo! hurrah! hurrah! Long live the daughter of England!" As the cannonade increased instead of diminishing,' he goes on, 'this gave a kind of martial note of approval to our solemn and enthusiastic ceremony.'

P. M. declared that he meant to run the whole way back, but on Soyer remarking that in that case the Russians would take him for a deserter and shoot him down, he walked with the others, crying out in disgust, 'You may say what you like about bravery—let me tell you, Monsieur Soyer, that I did not bargain for being brave, and I think the sooner we get out of this the better. Only listen to the roaring of the cannon!' They reached the sentry safely, and were told that many 'amateurs' came up to look at Sebastopol from the battery, and that the Russians never fired at them if there was a lady in the party. *Tempora mutantur* . . . .

Trying to find a short cut through the camp on the way back, they lost themselves. A Zouave showed them their road, and advised them to hurry, as the camp was full of thieves, and his colonel had threatened to lock up any strangers found loitering after dusk. Soyer and P. M. fell behind and lost their friends; P. M. began to see brigands in every bush, and to wish that some colonel *had* arrested him and locked him up safely for the night. Figures loomed up in the darkness and ordered them to halt. But instead of brigands ready to slit their throats, these were friendly Zouaves who warmed them with hot coffee before pointing out the best path to the port. Soyer was calm enough to taste the drink critically, remarking that it was very good, though hardly sweet enough, and despite P. M.'s pleas for haste, he stopped to enquire how rations of sugar were issued in the French army.

But after such a day even Soyer was glad to find himself at last back on board, and he fell asleep immediately despite the hardness of his narrow berth.

Plans were easily made. Their carrying-out was quite another matter, as Soyer found out next day at the Sanatorium. Captain King, the chief engineer, was suspicious of this flamboyant foreigner. 'You are aware', he said, 'that we are not in London, and I cannot build a kitchen such as you had at the Reform Club.' Soyer laughed. 'I should be very sorry if you could,' he answered, 'as in that case you would have to get somebody else to manage it, for I assure you I would not like to begin my gastronomic career again; and I must say I feel every bit as proud in having to cook for the soldiers, if not more so, than ever I did in cooking for the greatest epicures or the first lords of England.' 'Then,' said Captain King, much mollified, 'we shall work well together.' Soyer lamented the non-arrival of his stoves, which would have obviated the need for buildings, but explained how simple his requirements were. Miss Nightingale and her staunch ally, Dr Sutherland, one of the sanitary commissioners, approved Soyer's plans as models for all further kitchens needed, and Soyer thought that now all was well.

Two days later his complacency was rudely shattered when Miss Nightingale told him that not a single man was at work on his kitchens—they said they had no planks, and could not get any. Neither Miss Nightingale nor the purveyor could get anything done. Soyer rushed to Captain King's office, but could not find him there, or on the Heights, and only discovered that no steps had been taken to start work on the new buildings. The next day Soyer reached the site soon after daybreak; neither workmen nor captain appeared. Finally, Captain King was run to earth near his office—three tiny rooms up a tumble-down wooden staircase—outside which a long queue was waiting. Ignoring them, Soyer pursued Captain King into his inner room, locked the door and pocketed the key. 'For ten minutes', he said, 'you are my prisoner.' Again he produced his plans, explained that Lord Raglan himself had promised that they should be carried out, and demanded immediate action. Captain King insisted that he had neither the necessary materials nor the necessary workmen, but promised to do what he could, and with that Soyer had to be content.

Even if materials had been available, transportation was complicated by appalling weather. 'Three days of incessant rain', wrote a diarist. 'Oh how miserable everybody was! The ground ankle-deep in swamp...at every step the mud closes over your horse's fetlock joint,' and it had been in pouring rain that Soyer and Mr Bracebridge had ridden over —this time successfully—to see Lord Raglan. They met him, accompanied by many staff officers and Omar Pasha, the Turkish commander-in-chief, riding over to Balaclava to receive General della Marmora, who had just arrived at the head of the Sardinian contingent. Raglan remembered that Soyer had shown him over the Reform Club many years before; 'You have worked hard since then,' he said, 'and have got on in the world.' Soyer naturally replied that he was willing to work even harder under his lordship's orders.

Omar Pasha offended the *chef* by asking him if it was true that he had come to open an hotel in Eupatoria, but Raglan at once corrected him. 'M. Soyer has come to teach the soldiers how to make the best of their rations', he explained. 'They will not change their old style of cooking for anyone else. I, myself, and their colonels and even generals have taken a deal of interest and trouble in trying to teach them a better way of cooking. They adopt our plan while we are present, but when once our backs are turned, they go on in their old way.' 'Very true', said Omar Pasha. 'It is just the same with my men; show them anything better than their pilaff, they will not adopt it for the world.' Lord Raglan complimented Soyer on his work at Scutari, and told him that he was welcome to come to headquarters at any time, and that all his plans would receive official backing.

Meanwhile the 'Robert Lowe' had left the harbour, and Soyer had moved to the 'London', a vessel which had created a great sensation when launched in the middle of the eighteenth century. He arrived to spend his first night there very late, when everyone had turned in, and the lights were out. A sentry showed him his berth, and crawling into it as best he could, he fell asleep from weariness almost at once. He was wakened by hordes of rats racing about over his body, and finding it impossible to drive them away for more than a few moments, he retired to the main cabin and slept there as best he could on a bench. In the morning he found that the rats had eaten right through his greatcoat to get at a sample piece of Sardinian biscuit in one of the pockets. The next night he demanded, and was given, a different cabin, in which all the rat-holes had been stopped, and he was allowed, as a favour, a night-lamp. He shut the bull's-eye to prevent any rats escaping, and set about those in the cabin with a stick, making such a din that everyone was roused, and the captain, who was rather deaf, and half-asleep, told the mate to send for the police and have the drunken man turned out. All at once one of the rats, trying to escape, upset the lamp and extinguished it, so that once again Soyer had to take refuge in the main cabin.

Soyer himself must tell the next part of an astonishing story. 'The Captain made his appearance rather in a state of *négligé*, holding a rush-light in one hand and a sword in the other, with a nightcap tied with a red riband upon his head.' He enquired what the row was about, and Soyer explained that he had been trying to rid his cabin of rats. The Captain agreed that they were a great nuisance, '"They make quite as free in my cabin," he said, "but being used to it I do not care so much about them. The worst of it is that we can never keep a bit of cheese or a candle, they eat them up as fast as I buy them."

'"It is certainly very provoking, Captain; but why not try and catch them?"

'"Why, bless you, we have tried everything—poison, traps, broken glass. We caught a few, but I would give the world to have them all caught."

'"I can give you a receipt which will enable you to have them almost all caught in a few days."

'"The deuce you could!" said he, coming and sitting opposite to me. "Tell me how it is done—I shall be so much obliged to you; but I must go and put something on first, I am so cold." As he said this I perceived that the skylight over his head was open.

'"Oh never mind that, it won't take two minutes to tell you. Listen to me."

'"So I will", he said.

'"The place where you keep your cheese would be the very spot to make the trial. The thing is quite easy. Have your cheese and candles removed."

'"So I will; but I wish you would let me put a coat on—I am getting so very cold."

'"Never mind about that; I shall not keep you a minute—listen to me."

'"So I will."

'"When the cabin is perfectly empty, have it cleaned and scrubbed."

'"That will be done."

'"When it is dry, take half a pound of good Cheshire cheese, scrape it fine and mix it with about two pounds of bread-crumbs."

'"Yes I will."

'"Perhaps you think it a pity to give them half a pound of good cheese?"

'"Not at all, because the vermin eat pounds of it daily."

'"Mix both well together."

'"Yes, I understand, and make them into balls."

'"No, not at all—only spread the lot upon the floor, leave the doors and windows open, and go to bed. Of course they will come and eat."

'"I should say they would", he observed.

'"The next evening do the same, cutting the cheese a trifle larger. They will come again and eat it."

'"What next?" said he.

'"The third night, leave the doors and windows open; go to bed as usual, and put nothing at all in the cabin."

'"What then?" he asked again, in a state of anxiety.

'"Why, of course, when they come and find nothing to eat, and being in still greater numbers than the two previous nights, they will all be caught."

'"How", said he, "will they all be caught?"

'"Why, of course, finding nothing to eat, they will all be taken in!"

'"That be damned! I have made a nice fool of myself standing here half-naked to listen to such rubbish as that!"

'Having said that, he ran into his cabin, and for a long while I heard him sneezing and muttering to himself. The word "fool" was all that I could catch; and soon after all was silent till daybreak.'

Small wonder that when Soyer heard the Captain coming along to his cabin early next morning, he thought that a duel was the least satisfaction that would be demanded of him. But the Captain only begged him not to spread the story, partly so that the crew should not be able to laugh at their Captain, and partly so that he could play the joke himself on his friends! For days afterwards whenever they met the Captain would say to Soyer, 'Who caught the rats?' and Soyer would answer, 'You mean, who caught the Captain who could not smell a rat?'

Soyer's plans were always approved by those in authority, but not by any means always put into practice at once. The naval hospital in Leander Bay, however, was an exception—there any suggestions he made were at once carried out. With Miss Nightingale and several doctors Soyer paid this hospital a visit of inspection, and then they all scattered for a walk. The ground was lovely with flowers, and when the party reassembled, it was found that each gentleman had collected a bouquet for Miss Nightingale, who had to decide which of the half-dozen she would accept. For a moment the stern administrator vanishes, and a glimpse is caught of Miss Nightingale of Lea Hurst at a picnic. But on the way back she insisted on visiting the General Hospital, to enquire after a patient, and Soyer met her 'coming down the hill... walking through the mud in thin boots'. 'I could not refrain', he says, 'from expressing my fear that she would catch cold.' Miss Nightingale's only answer was an enquiry as to the progress of one of his kitchens.

Among the many problems which faced the commandant of Balaclava, Colonel Hardinge, the most pressing was still that of the supply of fuel. To get it brought as far as Balaclava he had to organise a fleet of ships, then he had to find men to unload the fuel, space to store it, and means of transporting it to all the different regiments and hospitals. When Hardinge realised the saving in fuel which could be brought about by the adoption of Soyer's stove, he naturally became very enthusiastic about it; thus encouraged, the inventor took his model to Lord Raglan. The commander-in-chief was so interested that he sent for Omar Pasha to inspect it also, but the Turkish commander, though civil and admiring, obviously felt that his men would never abandon their braziers for any such contrivance. Lord Raglan promised once more that the engineering department should be ordered to give Soyer's plans priority, and then suggested that among the kitchens in need of improvement was his own at headquarters. He overwhelmed Soyer by asking for the receipt of the *pot-au-feu* served at the Reform Club, which he had remembered with pleasure for fourteen years.

Armand, Lord Raglan's *chef*, received Soyer in 'what he called his kitchen, though it had not the slightest claim to the title, as it was all but destitute of culinary utensils', and the visitor compared it unfavourably with the kitchen at French headquarters. Mere cooks, however, could not complain, for at the beginning of the campaign 'it was no uncommon thing for a general to rest from the fatigues of war in a small dilapidated room something like a good-sized English pig-sty', and the headquarters of all the medical departments—Dr Hall's quarters—were in a hut 'about ten feet square, the height of a sentry-box, affording about enough room for four persons to stand up and for only two to sit down'.

Despite Hall's hatred and distrust of outsiders sent out by the Government, whom he classed as 'pathologists, sanitary commissioners, and I don't know what 'issioners, with high salaries and no occupation...female Inspectors and Directors of Nurses and I don't know what beside', he seems to have received Soyer kindly enough, offering to send a pony to fetch him from Balaclava, so that they could inspect the field kitchens together.

All plans, however, were cancelled by news which appalled the whole army. Miss Nightingale suddenly developed a severe form of Crimean fever, and was not expected to live. A file of soldiers carried her up to the Sanatorium, while P. M. held a white umbrella over her head, and her little drummer boy, Thomas, who always called himself 'Miss Nightingale's man', brought up the rear of the procession sobbing bitterly. All work, except that on the kitchen at the Sanatorium, seemed to come to a standstill, and as the news spread enquiries and expressions of sorrow came in from everyone, from Lord Raglan himself to the privates who had known her at Scutari. When at last it was learnt that she was out of danger, everyone rejoiced, and Soyer joyfully climbed to the Genoese Heights every day, to cook some special dish to tempt the invalid's appetite. The kitchen at the Sanatorium was finished, and the soldier-cooks who had been trained at Scutari ran it very efficiently.

At last, Soyer felt, his work was beginning to have some results.

CHAPTER XIV

CULINARY CAMPAIGN: VIDI

'Next, he was at war, turning the tides of it to victory for his own land by meals of bacon and eggs that brought bemedalled Generals in troops like Pelicans, to his fireplace.' KIPLING, *His Gift*

ADMIRAL BOXER was in charge of the port of Balaclava. Luckily his energy and cheerfulness were almost inexhaustible, for his duties were many and his worries innumerable. 'From daybreak to sunset he might be seen rowing about like a hunted pirate', says Soyer. Many years before, the admiral had bought and treasured one of the *chef*'s books, and now he found its author a man after his own heart. The chronic confusion in the harbour was increased, if possible, by the arrival of the Sardinians, and Boxer decided that the only way to disembark them was to build a bridge over the 'London', and march men and horses to shore over it. Of course Soyer had to point out how curious it was, while in the Crimea, to see a Sardinian army crossing London Bridge, and the joke pleased the admiral. Being besieged by Sardinian officers with all sorts of enquiries and complaints, he asked Soyer to act as interpreter; 'But pray', he said, 'don't tell them who I am, or they will worry my life out.'

When Boxer was called away, he left Soyer to deal as best he could with the more or less mutinous crowd. Their horses had not been watered, and they refused to take them ashore until this was done. Soyer told them that the only water available was 'soda-water'; they declared that *any* water would do, and were naturally furious when he produced some bottles and they discovered what it was. He immediately produced glasses and sherry also, and persuaded them to slake their own thirst, then kept them laughing till waterskins and

162

leather buckets arrived for the horses. Single-handed, as he told his friends afterwards, he calmed an army, and quelled the great Sardinian insurrection.

The hospital kitchens most in need of reformation were those of the General Hospital before Sebastopol. This hospital had to deal with any sudden influx of wounded after an action, but it was so badly fitted out that even the comparatively small number of wounded and sick received daily were half-starved. Dr Mouatt, in charge of it, received Soyer again and again, commended his schemes, approved his plans, and listened politely to his protests and demands, but nothing was done. Soyer found, as Colonel Windham had, that 'there appeared to be a perfect paralysis when any plain little com-monsense thing was proposed'. One difficulty after another hindered the work, and eventually Soyer, to his great chagrin, had to return to Scutari while Dr Mouatt was still waiting for the ordnance department to supply him with bricks.

The commissioners sent out by the Government to investi-gate conditions at the front were trying to organise bakeries at Balaclava, so that the sick at least should have bread instead of biscuit, and co-opted Soyer. When the bakeries on board the 'Abundance' and the 'Bruiser' were ready, Soyer as usual made the opening day the occasion for a reception, which so crowded the ships that the captain in charge complained he would never be able to make a fair start. Soon they were turning out between fifteen and sixteen hundred rations daily, and when additional bakeries at Kadekoi, a village a mile from the port, were finished also, enough bread was being made to give rations to all the men four times a week.

Soyer invented a kind of bread-biscuit, which stored well, yet was infinitely more palatable than the iron-hard ration biscuit, and which made, when soaked in tea, coffee or soup, a substantial and pleasant dish. The commissioners recom-mended it for general use, and were delighted too with his substitute for the dried vegetables which were by this time being issued twice a week. These ration packets of dried vegetables were certainly better than nothing, but as each packet contained enough for three days, the men were apt to cook more than they could eat on the day of issue, and have nothing left for the other days. Soyer planned to have mixed dried vegetables compressed into cakes, divided into sections like blocks of chocolate, so that the exact daily ration could easily be broken off. Commissary Filder approved in principle, but as ever was unwilling to take steps to carry out the change. The indefatigable Soyer gave him no peace until orders for the new vegetable cakes were sent home, and by the end of July they were a regular issue, much welcomed by the troops, as during the hot weather the fresh vegetables which now came up weekly from Constantinople often arrived half-rotten.

Filder was also bullied and persuaded to have the meat issued the night before it was to be cooked—the simplest of reforms, but most important, for it meant that the excess of salt which so often made the meat uneatable could be soaked out during the night. Even then there was delay until every regiment could be supplied with tubs in which to do the soaking.

Soyer was always on the move from kitchen to kitchen. 'From the peculiarity of my costume', he writes, 'I was almost as well-known to everyone in camp as a *chien du régiment*.' It was not only his practical successes which made him popular; it was cheering merely to see that extraordinary figure, so fantastically dressed, always hurrying along, always with fifty things on hand, but never too busy to jump from his pony to taste a stew, or improve the draught of a camp kitchen, always laughing and joking and cracking outrageous puns. He was showered with invitations to dine, and with offers of lodging for the night and ponies for his ceaseless journeyings.

One morning he borrowed a grey pony from Dr Hadley of the Sanatorium, in order to ride over to the camp. Hadley jokingly begged him to take care of himself, and of the pony, and above all of the beautiful new English saddle, which was absolutely irreplaceable; shouting back reassuringly that he would be back with the saddle at least for supper at seven, Soyer set off down the slippery path from the Genoese Heights to the port.

The streets were so thronged that it took him half an hour to push the few hundred yards through the town. Free at last, he rode briskly along the road to the camp, when suddenly he was hailed by a crowd of officers standing at the door of the 'British Hotel'. This was the remarkable unofficial canteen owned by Mrs Seacole, a prodigiously fat and immensely good-natured old woman, who had known in her native Jamaica many of the officers now in the Crimea. She came to the door at the noise of an arrival, crying 'Who is my new son'? to which one of the officers replied, 'Monsieur Soyer, to be sure. Don't you know him?' 'God bless me, my son, are you Monsieur Soyer of whom I heard so much in Jamaica? Well to be sure!' She declared that she had sold many and many a score of his Relish and other sauces, and could sell more still if she could only get them fast enough. The jolly old creature was high in favour with all her 'Jamaica sons', and they easily persuaded Soyer to dismount and have a drink with them.

He was invited into the tin hut, where she asked his advice about the stocking of her canteen, and when at length he emerged, in a hurry to be off and make up for lost time, he found his pony gone, and no sign of it anywhere. Mother Seacole made a great fuss, declared that every pony in sight must be the missing one, and promised to send its description round all the regiments. (It was owing to her enquiries that the pony was eventually recovered ten days later.) Meanwhile she lent Soyer another pony owned by her partner Mr Day, and advised him to go to the 'Hue-and-Cry' at headquarters to make enquiries.

The postmaster there, Mr Angel, invited Soyer to stay to

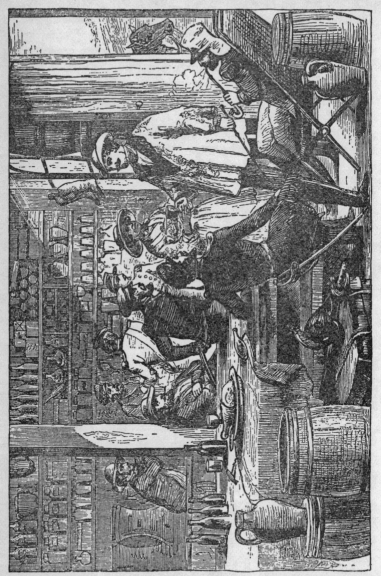

Mrs Seacole and Soyer in the 'British Hotel'

dinner, and brushed aside excuses, saying that there was an empty hut to sleep in, and that the renowned Mr Russell was to be the guest of honour. Having ridden round the camp for an hour, searching in vain for his mount, Soyer accepted the invitation on the rather ingenuous grounds that he could thus be on the spot to look for his pony in the morning; he had apparently quite forgotten Dr Hadley and his friends at the port.

What a dinner it was! The six guests sat down at a table which was astonishingly equipped with real knives and forks, real plates, and even a real tablecloth. They had 'very strong preserved soup, a very nice tough fowl', and the rest of the dinner was made from ration meat. There was abundant drink, and soon the party began to sing choruses. More and more people joined them, and Lord Raglan sent to enquire what all the noise was about. (Soyer explains carefully that after explanations Lord Raglan said that he enjoyed the singing, and that they were not to be disturbed.) By ten o'clock, which in the Crimea was equivalent to twelve or one in London, complaints about the noise began to come from neighbouring tents. Those who complained were invited to join the party, but Mr Angel, saying that they were all playing the devil with his cellar, told the newcomers to go back and bring their own drinks. This rowdy bottle-party went on till midnight, when the guests dispersed as steadily as they might.

After this 'regular London evening', as Soyer describes it, he woke up to find himself 'wrapped in a horse-cloth, with a pair of top-boots for pillow'. Going stiffly to reclaim Mr Day's pony, which he had left with Lord Raglan's groom, he found the owner riding off on it, very cross because it had not been returned the night before. Undaunted, Soyer borrowed yet another mount, this time from Lord Raglan, and proceeded on his search. First he persuaded one of General Canrobert's aides-de-camp to advertise his loss through the French camp, then he breakfasted at a French canteen, and spent some time inspecting their camp kitchens. He decided that despite the praises lavished on the French system, his new stoves would feed the English army better still, and for the thousandth time he longed for their arrival.

All enquiries about the pony were fruitless, but there was a rumour that some regiment on Cathcart's Hill had found a grey. Search on the spot brought no result; he met there, however, Sir John Campbell, who remarked that his kitchen was sadly inadequate. Sir John bewailed the dullness of everlasting boiled ration meat at every meal, so Soyer set to and concocted a savoury stew, and assured Sir John that in a couple of hours—if not allowed to boil—it would be a dish fit for the gods, or the most particular of generals. Refusing to stay and share it, as he ought to get on to Balaclava, Soyer was about to leave, when flags of truce appeared, to enable both sides to collect and bury their dead.

He decided to seize the opportunity of seeing Sebastopol at close quarters, and entrusting his pony to a Zouave, set out on foot towards the Russian lines. The ground was seamed with ravines, and he wandered to and fro, finally getting thoroughly lost in the French trenches. Emerging in the gathering dusk, he tried to find the place from which he had set out, but strayed into No Man's Land, from which a sentry called him back just in time. When after much trouble he found his pony, he had no idea where he was, and falling in with a French regiment coming out of the front line, he rode after them to their quarters. He spent a pleasant and hilarious evening in their canteen, and slept on some straw on the floor, passing—in his own words—'a noisy night', with 'shots hissing overhead'.

He left the canteen at six the next morning, and was back in Balaclava by eight, having visited on the way the Turkish and Sardinian camp kitchens. His absence had caused a crop of wild rumours—that he had lost three horses—that he had lost himself—that he had last been seen going towards the Russian lines at dusk—that he was missing—even that he had been taken prisoner. Mr Bracebridge and Thomas (the head cook) were scouring the camp for him, while P. M. in the telegraph office composed telegrams of enquiry to send to headquarters.

Fortunately, Soyer arrived in time to cancel the telegrams, and asked P. M. to go instead to Dr Hadley—who had already learnt of his pony's fate from Mrs Seacole's enquiries—with Soyer's profoundest apologies. Off went P. M. on Lord Raglan's pony, which he had borrowed to save time. He had not gone far when a zealous military policeman, espying 'L. R. Headquarters' marked on the pony's side, arrested him, crying out that here was the pony stolen from M. Soyer, about which so much fuss had been made. P. M. protested violently but uselessly, until a passing officer who knew him identified him as Soyer's secretary; then he was released, but had to trudge up to the Sanatorium on foot, as the policeman insisted on keeping his steed.

This affair of the ponies became a standing joke. The story was that Soyer had lost three horses, and his secretary one, none of them their own property. Soyer was not at all annoyed; on the contrary, he maintained that any fool could lose his own horse, but that it required a good deal of skill and standing in society to lose four belonging to other people in so short a time. When Colonel Hardinge was next asked to lend Soyer a mount, he sent his charger—on the grounds that it would be less easily lost—which promptly ran away with the *chef*, though luckily not in the direction of Sebastopol.

Mrs Seacole when writing of her adventures in the Crimea gave her impression of 'the great high priest of the mysteries of cookery, Mons. Alexis Soyer', who visited her 'with the most smiling of faces and in the most gorgeous of irregular uniforms, and never failed to praise my soups and dainties. I always flattered myself', she said, 'that I was his match, and with our West Indian dishes could of course beat him hollow, and more than once I challenged him to a trial of skill; but the gallant Frenchman only shrugged his shoulders, and disclaimed my challenge with many flourishes of his jewelled hands, declaring that Madame proposed a contest where victory would cost him his reputation for gallantry, and be more disastrous than defeat.... Then he would laugh and declare that, when our campaigns were over, we would render rivalry impossible, by combining to open the first restaurant in Europe. There was always fun in the store when the good-humoured Frenchman was there.'

The queen's birthday, on 24th May, was celebrated by the dressing out of all the ships in the harbour with flags, and by the firing of a royal salute. Despite the heat, the sailors were feasted on roast beef, plum pudding and rum, and Soyer was invited to dinner on the 'Triton'. His party was broken up early by a gruesome discovery; an unpleasant smell round the ship was found to be caused by the bodies of those who had been drowned in the 'Prince'[1] in November. These had been buried at high-water mark, and partially uncovered by the tide; their reburial was no one's business, for Colonel Hardinge had jurisdiction only over dry land, and Admiral Boxer had no authority above the level of the water.

Occasionally, Soyer managed to take a night off; he spent one jovial evening with the 11th Hussars, some of whom he had known at Scutari. The dinner seemed luxurious, because there were enough knives and forks to go round, and, too, because 'good health—a ferocious appetite—lots of capital ale, porter, sherry, port, champagne—laughter, puns and fun in abundance—witty anecdotes and plenty of songs, good bad and indifferent, prevailed'. But the war could not be forgotten, even for one evening: returning from his feast at midnight, Soyer met a sad procession going to the hospital. A young Sardinian officer with cholera was being carried to the English hospital because their own was full. Soyer went with the stretcher-bearers to show them the best way, and finding that

[1] The 'Prince', laden with stores of all kinds, had been sunk just outside Balaclava harbour by a great storm.

no one else could translate the officer's last wishes, stayed with him all night till he died.

Ten days after his adventures with the pony, Soyer got hold of a splendid piece of beef—a rare thing to find in the Crimea. He decided to present it to Lord Raglan, and sent Thomas ahead on foot carrying the beef, while he followed on horseback as escort. Soyer stopped for a moment to thank Mother Seacole for her help in recovering Dr Hadley's pony, and Thomas disappeared in the distance. His anxious master overtook him just in time to save the beef from a Zouave's *popotte*; Thomas was drinking brandy with a group of Zouaves, and had unwrapped his treasure for their examination and admiration. They edged closer and closer to him, saying, 'Anglais roast-beef—bono johnny', and patting his back. As one of them stretched out his hand to seize the prize, Soyer spurred up to them, crying in French, 'How dare you stop drinking this way, Thomas, when you know that General Canrobert must have this beef for dinner, and it is already after three?' 'Oh', said a Zouave, 'it's no go, it's for the general.' The bewildered Thomas began to ask what on earth his master meant, but Soyer hurried him away—'Get along with you! No, I had better take it myself'—and chuckling at his success he trotted off clasping the precious beef.

Armand, Lord Raglan's *chef*, swore that he had not seen such a piece of meat for months, and was bidden to take good care of it now he had it; necessary advice, as a whole sheep had vanished mysteriously from the larder a few days before, and thirty live sheep and mules had been stolen within the week. Lord Raglan himself inspected the gift, saying that it would prove a test for Armand, and quoting Brillat Savarin— 'On devient cuisinier; mais on naît rôtisseur.' The general was something of a gourmet, and had been a friend of Lord Alvanley, when the latter lodged with Ude.[1] Lord Raglan recalled some stories about the old *chef*. Years before, Ude had been asked to find a cook for Raglan's brother, the Duke

[1] See p. 16.

of Beaufort. 'Ude called several mornings', said Lord Raglan, 'first with two dogs, then three, then four. At last I said to him, "I am very obliged to you, Mr Ude, for your kind visits respecting my brother's cook, and shall be happy to see you at any time, but in future without your four-legged companions!"

'"Why?" asked the great *chef*, rather put out.

'"My dear sir, if you want an explanation, enquire of the housemaid!" He rushed out, and never called again, but he sent the cook all the same.'

Gourmet as he had been in England, Lord Raglan's kitchen at headquarters in camp was very poorly equipped, and he fed little better than anyone else. Eager to do everything he could to improve the soldiers' food, he always encouraged and assisted Soyer. Mrs Davis noted that Lord Raglan used to visit the hospital about three times a week, and always inspected her kitchens and the food given to the patients, telling her to be sure to add plenty of wine to the arrowroot, for the country grudged nothing to the soldiers.[1] Those at home who censured the commander, and blamed him for the terrible starvation during the winter, had no idea of the difficulties with which he had to cope, not the least of which was the tendency of his staff to conceal from him the worst truths.

During the summer, expeditions became the fashion, and 'amateurs', as they were called, came out from England to inspect the scene of battle. Soyer received hundreds of invitations—some of them not entirely disinterested, for it was becoming well known that rather than sit down to an indifferent meal Soyer would cook a better one himself. He spent one care-free day on an expedition to the beautiful newly captured country in the Kamara mountains, and the Tchernaya valley, but his rounds of the new kitchens, his

---

[1] She declared that after his death she never saw a staff officer anywhere near the kitchens.

special cooking for Miss Nightingale, his lessons to the soldier-cooks and a thousand other duties kept him employed from dawn till late at night, and almost every invitation had to be refused.

Still there was no word of the arrival of the new stoves, and Mr Bracebridge grew impatient. He tried to convert some old round stoves he had found on a scrap heap into field stoves on Soyer's model, with locally made tin pans which were, though absurdly expensive, of the poorest quality. Soyer willingly helped him to exhibit them at headquarters, but they were so obviously makeshift that Lord Raglan decided to wait until the *chef*'s own samples arrived. Eventually, news came that the stoves had been delivered at Scutari, and Soyer made up his mind to go down and fetch them himself. This was all the more necessary as Jullien, the cook whom he had left there in charge, had fallen ill, and had written several times to say that he was determined to go home.

Miss Nightingale was getting stronger, and was most unwilling to leave the Crimea, saying that her work there had only just begun, but her doctors insisted that she should go at least to Scutari to rest for a time. A transport was chosen to convey her, but it had been used to bring up horses, and the smell was so horrible that she fainted almost as soon as she was carried on board. Lord Ward then put his yacht at her disposal, and with Soyer and Mr Bracebridge she was taken back to Scutari in it. Soyer was disgusted to find the passage so rough that he could not even taste the excellent meals prepared by Lord Ward's *chef*.

When they reached the calmer waters of the Bosphorus, Miss Nightingale was carried on deck, and Soyer hastened to ask after her health. She dismissed the matter, politely but quite firmly, and began at once to discuss the improvement of the extra-diet kitchens. It was useless for Soyer to assure her that he would report to her every day, that she must rest, that her own health must be considered; while she could think at all she thought of her work.

Soyer was considered lucky to have a kiosque at Scutari reserved for his own use, though it was not by any means a model dwelling. The rats which had lived in it during his absence were only evicted after a hunt lasting several days, followed by extensive hole-stopping. The landlord, a Turkish carriage-builder, lived and worked on the ground floor. He rose at 4 a.m., and with his four assistants started a continuous hammering immediately under Soyer's bedroom; this was bad enough, but the monotonous and noisy song to which they hammered was quite unbearable. The boards of the bedroom floor were sieve-like, and the workers found that the beginning of song was accompanied by various 'accidental' spillings of large buckets of water above, which drenched them and made them change their tune. Through his Armenian groom the *chef* threatened that unless they were quieter the general would turn them out of the house, and this combination of physical and moral suasion proved fairly effective.

The strong morning sea-breeze rocked the crazy building and blew the branches of the cherry and mulberry trees in front of it almost into the first-floor rooms. One evening as Jullien the head cook was singing there with some friends, the branches swung right into the room, and knocked their glasses and bottles off the table. P. M. cried out in fright, but Jullien said, 'Don't be alarmed, it's only an earthquake.' '*Only* an earthquake', exclaimed P. M., bolting. Rushing out of the door he collided with a servant bringing in a bowl of blazing punch, set himself alight, and disappeared downstairs in a halo of flame. Next day he reappeared, unhurt, explaining that he had thought it better to be swallowed at one gulp by the yawning earth than to be crushed bit by bit by the timbers of the kiosque.

The 11th Hussars invited Soyer to a very merry dinner at which the guest of honour was Selim Pasha, the Governor of Asia Minor. Paying his respects to the great man some days later, the *chef* was received with much honour. The Pasha took his hand, and the interpreter warned Soyer on no account to pull it away until it was released by his host. A cry of 'Fire!' was heard in the street, and the Pasha strode up and down giving orders, still holding his embarrassed guest firmly by the hand. At last Soyer found himself free, and tried to take his leave, but to his horror the Pasha again seized him—luckily by the other hand this time—and asked for the pleasure of his company as far as Lower Scutari, where all the minarets were illuminated for the feast of Ramazan. Horses were waiting, but the dragoman whispered that his highness wished to do his guest great honour, and would walk hand-in-hand with him through the town. For some two miles they walked at the head of a brilliant procession, and Soyer writes that he had often to remind himself that in reality he had 'a humble part to play on life's great stage', as all the soldiers presented arms, and the dense crowds parted, bowing, to make way for the Pasha and his honoured guest.

A few days later, at a five-hour banquet given by the same Pasha, the main dish was of sheep and lambs roasted *à la Turque*, that is, cooked whole and eaten with the fingers. Soyer was allowed to visit the kitchen and inspect the process, which cooked the meat so perfectly that 'every part of the animals was the colour of a lump of gold'.

These entertainments were mere interludes in a busy life. The new arrangements at the hospitals had worked admirably during Soyer's absence, though Jullien complained bitterly that no sooner had he got a cook shaping well than the man was sent back to his regiment and succeeded by a complete novice. The only serious complaints came from the officers in the Palace Hospital at Hyder Pasha, where the patients did not find the pleasant tenor voice in which the steward sang to them sufficient consolation for the unripe fruit and rotten vegetables with which he fed them. The kitchen was rebuilt, a civilian cook was put in charge, and the steward dismissed. The officers rewarded Soyer's exertions with so many invitations to dine that he declared he could have satisfied three or four appetites daily.

One day one of the head cooks, who had been leading an agitation for higher wages, vanished with his subordinates just before dinner-time, without any warning. Soyer could not understand this behaviour; it was as shameful to him as the desertion of a general on the eve of battle, and though luckily he heard of the plot in time to take charge himself, the incident depressed him. He records sadly that this was 'one of the hundreds of tribulations and disappointments I met with during my Eastern mission'.

The new stoves were unpacked and demonstrated with great éclat; the inventor was complimented on them by no less a personage than the late Minister for War, the Duke of Newcastle, then on a visit to Constantinople. Jullien had left, and Soyer himself was 'manipulating some hundreds of mock rice puddings', when suddenly the kitchen was invaded by a group of officers, led by the duke, who advanced without ceremony and praised the *chef* very heartily for all his work in the East.

Two tolerably good cooks were found to replace Jullien, and a dozen soldiers were taught how to use the new stoves. These men were to accompany Soyer up to the Crimea, and 'Captain Cook'—as they called him—completed his brigade by engaging as aide-de-camp, *écuyer*, master of the horse and bodyguard a Zouave whose term of service had expired. This François Pitifal Bornet was a capital shot and an excellent horseman; he was expert at *la savate*, skilled with single-stick, sword and foil, and could box well; he could sing hundreds of songs, and danced excellently. His master was to discover later that he was also 'very quarrelsome, a great marauder *à la Zouave*; remarkably fond of the fair sex, running all over the camp after the heroic *cantinières*; though never drunk, seldom sober', and always ready to fight anyone in his master's interests.

CHAPTER XV

CULINARY CAMPAIGN: VICI

'So they drank to his health, and they gave him three cheers,
   While he served out additional rations.'
                LEWIS CARROLL, *The Hunting of the Snark*

IT was a cosmopolitan company which set out for the Crimea
at the beginning of August 1855. Under the command of an
Anglicised Frenchman were united an Armenian groom, a
Sardinian servant Antonio, the Zouave Bornet, the Englishman
P. M., M. Mesnil the major-domo, and T. G. the 'gentleman
of colour' who had been with the *chef* from the beginning.
Little wonder that this party 'always created a sensation
throughout the camp'. T. G. wore white, the Zouave flaunted
his bright uniform (Soyer had made 'some stylish improvements' in the regulation costume), while P. M. affected 'a
peculiar costume of nankeen'. Their leader was described in
a despatch of Russell's, who was showing John Bull round the
camp. 'I beg your pardon', said John Bull, 'but who is that
foreign officer in a white burnous and attended by a brilliant
staff of Generals—him with the blue and silver stripe down
his trousers I mean, and gold braid on his waistcoat, and a red
and white cap; it must be Pélissier?'—'*That*! Why that's
M. Soyer, *chef de nos batteries de cuisine*, and if you go and
speak to him you'll find he'll talk to you for hours about the
way your meat is wasted.'

Though he had been away barely a month, Soyer found that
he had to introduce himself all over again in the Crimea.
Admiral Boxer, Adjutant-General Estcourt, Sir John Campbell, and Lord Raglan himself, were dead. 'It strikes us',
wrote an officer's wife, 'that Death has taken the recall of
those in authority into his own stern hands.'

During this visit Soyer lived partly on board and partly under canvas. For the first trial of the stoves on a large scale, a spot was chosen on the esplanade in the middle of the camp; the stoves were duly sent up, but seemed to have disappeared on arrival; it was discovered that the Highland Brigade had already appropriated them, and that the men were using them to cook the day's dinner. After this no more was heard of the theory that the men would be unwilling to change their cooking utensils and manner of cookery—an objection to the stoves which had often been put forward by the more conservative officers.

The old method of cooking in small camp kettles over enormous open fires demanded a supply of several hundred-weights of fuel daily for each fire: the stove used approximately twelve pounds of coal, fifteen of coke or twenty of wood. The First Battalion of the Coldstream Guards, for instance, on the first day they had the stoves, used only 47 pounds of wood instead of the usual 1760, and only two cooks instead of sixteen. In general use, allowing twenty stoves to a regiment, the consumption would be three hundred pounds per thousand men; the old allowance was three and a half pounds per man, and the stoves thus saved three thousand two hundred pounds of fuel per regiment daily. In a smaller size, the same stove was especially useful in the trenches, because no fire showed even when cooking was going on.

The grand demonstration took place on the afternoon of 27th August. Lord Stratford had distributed the Order of the Bath in the morning, and most of the officers, as General Barnard said, devoted the morning to the *cordon rouge* and the afternoon to the *cordon bleu*, thus ensuring a fine show of uniforms at Soyer's *fête champêtre*, as he called it. He arranged to have a band playing, and ordered quantities of extra wine at his own expense. The usual Crimean difficulties—lack of carpenters, shortage of wood, want of transport carts—were overcome, and several marquees were erected to shelter the guests.

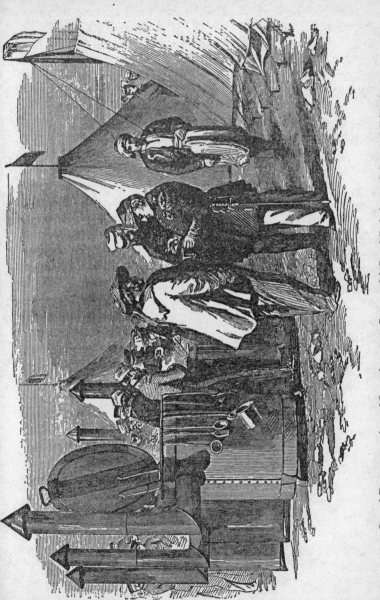

Grand Demonstration of Soyer's stove: Soyer with Lord Rokeby and General Pélissier
(from *The Illustrated London News*)

The Times correspondent sent home a full account. 'In the afternoon', he wrote, 'Soyer, the Gastronomic Regenerator, now the camp cook *par excellence*, opened the fire of his kitchens.... A huge row of boilers supplied each one its different soup or stew, concocted entirely from the rations daily furnished to the troops. From the summit of a large marquee fluttered the French and English colours; smaller flags waved gaily over the enclosure, which was formed by garlands of foliage. The guests, who were very numerous, paid due homage to the contents of the savoury cauldrons, the capacity of which alone saved them from speedy exhaustion. There was no denying the excellence of the cookery. Five o'clock is a hungry hour in the Crimea; and I can answer for it that few of the guests contented themselves with merely tasting. General Simpson[1] smiled approvingly at the skill of the French cook, and General Pélissier seemed highly to enjoy his countryman's *potage*.... There were rice pudding and Cossack plum-pudding (all rations), snug tents, with champagne and the most crystalline of ice (not rations) and Soyer was voted *nem. con.* the worthy *chef* of the army in the Crimea. To speak seriously, he will render real service if he teaches the soldier, as I understand he proposes to do, to make the most of the very excellent materials supplied to him, which hitherto have unquestionably been wasted, more or less, through ignorance of a few of the simplest laws of the gastronomic science.'

Compliments were heaped on the inventor, and he added to his ever-growing collection of testimonials letters of warm appreciation from Generals Simpson and Pélissier. Four hundred stoves, enough to supply the whole army, were ordered from home, and, lest cheap imitations should be sold to the public under his name, Soyer now took out a patent.

News of his success was spreading at home. Early in 1855 *Punch* had suggested that the Foreign Enlistment Bill should be used 'to enlist a few French cooks.... Let M. Soyer be

[1] Lord Raglan's successor.

empowered to raise a legion of them, and proceed at once to the Crimea with his culinary corps.' The advice had been taken, and now *Punch* dedicated to 'the Honourable Alexis Soyer' a ballad entitled *The Cordon Bleu*.

> The Cordon Bleu to the War is gone,
>   In the ranks of death you'll find him.
> His snow-white apron is girded on
>   And his magic stove behind him.
> 'Army beef,' says the Cordon Bleu,
>   'Though a stupid bungler slays thee,
> One skilful hand thy steaks shall stew,
>   One artist's pan shall braise thee.'
>
> Our cook went forth, and the foe in vain
>   On his pots and pans did thunder.
> He thicked thin gravy, he sauced the plain,
>   And he sliced coarse lumps asunder.
> And he cried, 'A Cook can defy, you see,
>   A Commissariat's knavery.
> The soldier who saves a Nation free,
>   Should have a ration savoury.'

Lord Panmure, worried by reports of drunkenness in the camp, suggested that Soyer should be consulted about the possibility of supplying the soldiers in the trenches, especially during the winter, with a pint of hot soup instead of the rum ration. Various generals met the *chef* for consultation, and most were in favour of supplying both soup and rum. Die-hard General Eyre dissented. 'I should be very happy', he said, 'to improve the daily food of the troops, but do not like anything to be overdone. I like judicious discipline in all things.' The generals were persuaded to visit one of the new field kitchens. 'M. Soyer gave us a most excellent luncheon', wrote General Windham, 'of which General Eyre partook most heartily, although he disapproved of the principle of Soyer's cooking.' 'Soldiers do not', said General Eyre, 'require such good messes as these while campaigning.' He ignored Soyer's pleas that the lunch had been cooked from the ordinary rations,[1] and that there had been great saving of fuel and labour, and exclaimed reproachfully as he rode away, 'You will improve the cook, but spoil the soldier.'

On 8th September the allies made a grand assault on Sebastopol, and next morning it was found that the Russians had retreated, abandoning the south side of the town. It was difficult to keep the Zouave Bornet out of the battle, 'the smell of gunpowder to him', says Soyer, 'was like the scent of a rat to a terrier', but he was needed as liaison officer between the *chef* and the hospitals. When in the evening wounded of all nationalities began to pour in, the hospital kitchens could not cope with the rush, and by four o'clock the next morning Soyer had begun to send up extra supplies from his kitchen in the camp. By nightfall all the wounded were under cover in the wards or in tents, and the tired *chef* accepted an invitation to dine with a group of officers at the 'Carlton Club'.

All had been engaged in the action, and when a servant rushed in crying that Sebastopol was in flames they all declared that they had seen enough of Sebastopol, that they were tired to death, and that nothing would induce them to go to Cathcart's Hill to view the burning city. Soyer was as exhausted as anyone, but he was never tired enough to forego a new experience. P. M. was so soundly asleep he could not be roused, Bornet too drunk, but Soyer managed to waken Mesnil, his major-domo, who, despite his cries of 'Hang the place! Let it burn!', was dragged out of bed. Together they climbed the hill, and watched the shooting flames and the dense clouds of smoke which hung over the city. Next day, accompanied by his Zouave, Soyer visited the still burning ruins, making straight for the kitchens of the barracks, where he tasted the black bread and *soupe-aux-choux* left by the Russians, and found them both exceedingly nasty.

[1] The only extra was ox-tail and ox-head soup, made from the heads and tails which had previously been buried as useless.

Bornet got leave to attend a friend's funeral, and did not come back for two days, when he arrived laden with trophies —a new tent, guns, swords, and every other kind of portable 'souvenir'. When reproved for his long absence, Bornet explained that after the funeral he had drowned his sorrows in drink. 'When I began to find', he explained, 'that I could no longer see, I said to myself, "Bornet my friend, you must not disgrace the governor's quarters. Go to bed upon the straw like the pig you are." In ten hours my drunken fit had passed away like a vaporous cloud; and here, governor, is your Zouave, fit as a fiddle, ready to dance upon a rope without a balance-pole.' This ingenious explanation turned his master's anger to laughter; Bornet was forgiven, and allowed to help with preparations for a great picnic which Soyer gave in the captured fortifications, where the Magic Stove performed its usual miracles.

Exhausted by his own lack of moderation in work and play, Soyer now became seriously ill with Crimean fever. No sooner was he allowed to rise than he tried to make up for his absence by extra exertions, and so brought on a second, and even more severe, attack. Three weeks later he was pronounced out of danger, but his appearance was so altered that he was hardly recognisable, and his friends declared that he had aged ten years in the last few months. Miss Nightingale had returned to the Crimea, and sent for him to help her at the hospitals; she was as unsparing of her subordinates as of herself, and he over-tired himself so seriously, attempting to carry out her plans, that he was ordered by the doctors to leave the Crimea at once.

A day or two later a correspondent of *The Illustrated London News* was resting in his tent, when 'a musical and hilarious voice exclaimed, "Is Guy Earl of Warwick at home?"' The visitor who burst in was astonished to see whose tent it was. '"Ah," he said, "I have made one grand mistake, you will think me strange. I was looking for my old friend Warwick, and made sure this was his tent...."' The correspondent saw that his visitor was 'a tall, stout, rather handsome-looking man, aged about fifty years. He wore a drab-coloured "wide-awake" wrapped round with a red scarf, and a white blouse, heavily braided about the sleeves. His hair had been black, now rapidly changing into grey; and his whiskers, moustache and beard (the latter primly cut) were of the same "Oxford mixture".'

They talked until the writer's servant brought in the dinner, a piece of beef baked in an iron pot, also some boiled potatoes. 'I observed', he goes on, 'that my visitor eyed the dinner curiously, and I was almost angry to observe the elevation of his eyebrows when with great difficulty I succeeded in whittling off with a sharp carving-knife a slice of the outside.

'"Nice beef, but not quite done enough", said my visitor.

'He might well say so; it was almost raw. I struck into the potatoes; they were as hard as pebbles.

'"I see you have a good fire outside", said my visitor. "That charcoal gives a beautiful heat. Now if you will take my advice, I should say, cut a slice or two—"

'"Excuse me", I replied, "but if there is one thing more than another that I pride myself on, it is my cooking. I can cook with any fellow in the Crimea, perhaps excepting Soyer; and some people say that he is a great humbug."

'"Do they indeed?" said he. "Well, he must be rather a clever humbug to sell forty thousand of his books!"

'"I must confess", I said, "that his Shilling Cookery Book is a great invention. I have made many capital dishes by its direction. The fact is, I generally superintend the cooking myself."

'"And your politeness to me has spoilt your dinner. Now look here." And almost before I could interpose a word, my potatoes were in slices, a large onion was dissected piecemeal, my beef was submitted to the knife, a pinch or two of ration salt and pepper completed the preparations, and my little canteen-pan was on the fire.... After a few minutes the stranger gave the pan a graceful wave or two over the fire, and then replaced it on the table. There was a dinner fit for Sardanapalus!...

'"How do you like it?" said the stranger.

'"Don't talk at present", I answered, "I consider dinner one of the most serious duties of life."

'"Ah! ah! then you would not call Soyer a humbug to make this?"

'"Soyer!" I said in disdain. "Soyer never made or invented a dish half so good in his life!"...At last dinner was over.

'"One more glass of sherry", said the stranger, "and then I go. I am very glad to have made your acquaintance, and I hope you will come and see me when you come down to Balaclava. I shall be on board the ship *Edward* in the bay. I am going to stop there a little time for my health. Come on board and ask for me."

'"With very great pleasure—and your name?"

'"Oh! my name—*Soyer*!" said he; and he sat down and laughed till the tears stood in his eyes.'

The Times—despite Russell's reputation for slashing criticism —had nothing but praise for Soyer's labours. Russell had welcomed Soyer's first visit to the front in May 1855 as holding out hopes of the establishment of 'some good and simple method of cooking and messing instead of the present very imperfect, irregular and wasteful system', and had reported the improvements in the hospitals as they slowly took place. In July he wrote that 'a better system has begun to prevail with regard to cooking', but in August he was still praising the 'snugly established' French and the 'extremely savoury odour coming from their crude but efficient kitchens'.

In October, General Simpson wrote to Panmure that 'the camps are getting a very comfortable set of kitchens'; in November, Russell declared that the English army was 'fed as no army was ever fed before', that the men were 'unmeasurably better off than their allies', and that it was common to see the latter 'eating in the English camps of the excess of our soldiers' cooking-kettles'. 'A true *entente cordiale*', he said, 'is established through the medium of the stomach.'

Panmure could now write to Codrington (Simpson's successor), and expect the suggestion to be carried out, that 'no man should leave his hut for work or duty without something warm to start with, such as soup, and the same waiting him on return'. The sick were now at last adequately nourished. 'The hospital kitchens', reported Russell, 'are certainly worth seeing, and M. Soyer has by the introduction of his stoves, and of an improved system of ménage, contributed to render them efficient. In economising fuel by the introduction of his stove, M. Soyer has rendered a considerable service. No article presses more heavily on the resources of the commissariat department, is more bulky and difficult of transport and more expensive, than wood for fuel.'

Everyone, in fact, was better off for Soyer's work—except himself. He was sent down to Scutari, and the doctors there ordered him to go straight home. He refused. His cooks had heard that he was dead, and were terrified when the worn and altered Soyer, a wraith of his former self, came into the kitchens. He became too weak to rise, and lay in 'Soyer House', with nothing to look at but the hospital on one side and the cemetery on the other. The weather was so bad, the house so crazy and the vermin so unbearable, that when his fever was complicated by dysentery he was moved to a hotel in Pera. Still he grew weaker, and still he refused to go home to England before his work was finished. His four hundred stoves were on the way out, and he was determined to remain alive long enough to distribute them to the different regiments, though Dr Sutherland told him bluntly that if he went back to the Crimea he had better take his tombstone with him.

For three months Soyer lay helpless; his recovery was thought impossible. But the advice of Vincent Ambler, a young surgeon, brought him to his feet again; once there, it was a mere step to a stove, and he swore his own cooking did more to cure him than the doctors. Soon he was going his rounds of the hospital kitchens once again. Rashly, against all advice, he insisted on attending a fancy-dress ball at the Embassy, declared that the sudden change of scene had worked a miraculous cure (despite a journey home in pouring rain in the small hours of the morning), and that he was now fit for anything.

Transport muddles were still frequent—Simpson wrote to Panmure in October, 'Huts are arriving, but sad complaints *still* come to me how difficult it is to find *in one ship* one complete hut.' The stoves were sent straight to Balaclava, and the ship did not call at Scutari to pick up Soyer. Hearing that the stoves had reached the front, Soyer hastily collected all his cooks—freed at last by the introduction of a medical staff corps in the hospitals—and for the third time left for the camp.

A hut had been built for him on Cathcart's Hill, in the midst of the Fourth Division, the cooking for which was entirely in his hands. At once, regiment by regiment, he began his cooking lessons. The first day that each kitchen had its stoves, Soyer himself instructed the cooks, and gave them printed directions and receipts. His civilian cooks helped and advised for the next few days, and he looked in at each kitchen for a moment or two as often as he could. As soon as a kitchen was working satisfactorily, he enquired of the officers, from the general commanding downwards, what they thought of it, and in this way he collected an enormous number of flattering testimonials. All told the same tale. 'They consume not a quarter so much fuel; they boil the meat more regularly, and the vegetables, and therefore make better soup; they never smoke, which is invariably the case with all barrack cookhouses. You can use them either out of doors or inside....'[1]

[1] General Lord William Paulet, commanding Light Division, June 1856.

So striking was this universal approval, that it was decided that the stove should be adopted by the entire army, at home and abroad, in peace and war, and Soyer determined to instruct in person as many regiments as possible. When peace was signed he realised that his time was short, and redoubled his efforts.

Peace brought other work too, of a new kind, for the end of the war was followed by an orgy of party-giving in the camp. The officers feasted their friends, their allies and their late enemies in banquets often designed, and on special occasions executed, by Soyer, and the men thronged the canteens. In place of earlier demands for funds to supply the army with bare necessities, *Punch* begged for contributions for a soda-water fund to relieve the morning hang-overs of Crimean heroes. Soyer was in demand as a guest as well as a *chef*, but on important occasions he often chose to supervise the work in the kitchen, appearing later to enjoy the diners' compliments, instead of sitting down himself.

One of his notable triumphs was the monster dish he provided at a few hours' notice when General Lüders (the Russian commander) visited and reviewed the French and English armies. It was an immense pyramid composed of lobsters, lampreys, sardines, anchovies, caviare, sturgeons, oysters, olives, mushrooms, truffles, a hundred eggs, and many other delicacies, topped by a card on which was written 'SOYER'S CULINARY EMBLEM OF PEACE, *the Macédoine Lüdersienne à la Alexandre II*', and was served on an inverted stove-lid, since no dish big enough could be found. Four commanders-in-chief, their staffs and over thirty other generals sat down to the luncheon, and only General Pélissier had any criticism to make; he complained that the olives were not stoned, and refused to accept Soyer's excuses. 'Oh!' exclaimed the *chef*. 'It is all very well for you to take the Malakhoff in a few minutes, but it took me four hours to make that dish!' Other successes were a *déjeuner* for Lüders's successor General Vassileffsky, with a most elaborate bill of fare; a banquet in honour of the Sardinian commander for which Soyer invented his *Crimean Cup à la Marmora*,[1] and a farewell dinner to Sir Colin Campbell on his departure for England.

Poor Soyer, still far from well, almost regretted the peace which brought such extra demands on his time and strength, but nevertheless he resolved to give a grand banquet in his own hut, 'Soyer's Villarette'; it was his last chance of getting his friends together before the armies were scattered over the world. The Crimean Madrigal Club, led by Colonel de Bathe, promised to attend and perform. The hut was carefully measured, and it was calculated that fifty guests might be squeezed in—fifty invitations were issued, and fifty acceptances were received.

The great day dawned cloudy and wet. Soyer was worried and nervous, feeling that this last feast must be perfect, for there would be no opportunity of blotting out mistakes by later successes. Two of his cooks were ill, and Colonel de Bathe called to say that two of the leading singers had left with their regiments, and the club felt it could hardly sing without them. While Soyer was reassuring him, and offering to sing himself if necessary, a messenger appeared with the news that the required knives and forks had not come back from a previous borrower, and that the special bread could not be baked in time. The ice ran short, and there was some doubt as to whether the promised band from the Rifles would turn up.

Soyer refused to be beaten. Half a dozen soldiers had searched the countryside for greenery, and the 'Villarette' was hung inside and out with bunches of flowers, green branches, lilac and evergreens, varied with small flags and red, blue, green and yellow paper lanterns. A friendly engineer designed and built an immense chandelier, and wax lights were put round in profusion. Twelve glass lamps—

[1] Still drunk with appreciation, for it is given with two other Crimean Cups in *A Gourmet's Book of Food and Drink*, John Lane, 1933.

procured with difficulty after much wire-pulling—were painted by a willing corporal with stripes of brightest blue, filled with ration fat for oil, and hung along the front of the hut. By mid-day the decorations were completed, and it only remained to clear the floor of 'half a ton of mud', carried in on the soldiers' boots, which, Soyer says, 'sadly interfered with the general appearance of the now enchanting spot'.

The turf outside, which had been specially laid a few days before, was burned dry and yellow by the sun, and it seemed impossible to get the planned effect of lamplight on green grass. Not at all. A pot or two of opal green paint was found, with a few amused soldier-painters, and soon the plot was greener than ever—so realistically green that some horses tethered close by broke their picket-ropes to reach it. This success seemed to change the whole spirit of the preparations. The crockery and cutlery, the bread and the ice turned up after all, two fresh waiters arrived, and a friend's cook volunteered as an assistant.

At nine o'clock all was ready. The tables glittered under the chandelier, the lamps blazed on the extraordinarily green turf, and the band played as the guests arrived. At half-past nine the concert began, madrigals and glees by the singers alternating with polkas and quadrilles by the band. At eleven the supper was served, the band still going strong. Lord Rokeby, the guest of honour, made a speech praising their host's work for the army, to which Soyer replied, in the words of *The Times*, 'with propriety and feeling'. Then the concert was resumed, while *punch à la Marmora* circulated freely. About two o'clock the senior officers left, and Soyer's own performance of a comic song was loudly encored by the crowd of spectators who had gathered outside the hut. The company gradually dwindled as the night passed, but at five o'clock there were still a few guests asking for their horses, and Soyer (even without the report which appeared in *The Times*) could rest assured that the last great party in the Crimea had also been the most successful.

VISITORS ARE
particularly requested
not to touch
The FLOWERS

H.S. HINE

A MODERN BOTANICAL GARDEN—NATURE OUTDONE.

Painting the Grass (from *Soyer's Culinary Campaign*)

Mr Ambler, the young surgeon who had cured Soyer at
Scutari, had himself been lying ill at Balaclava, and Soyer had
made daily visits with presents of delicacies. He was determined to have Ambler at his party, and though the doctor felt
himself too weak, Soyer insisted, and sent two men and a horse
to fetch him. The excitement laid Ambler up again—and
again Soyer began his daily visits of comfort!

A farewell performance was given in the theatre of the
Fourth Division, at which a Lance-Corporal of the 20th
Regiment, Thomas Price, sang a song of his own composition
in praise of the new stove.

> A trifling thing, gentlemen, I am going to mention;
> Oh tell me pray have you seen this great and new invention?
> To cook in camp I believe it is their intention;
> For Soyer's patent, I confess, it is a perfect creation.
> > Steam! Steam!
>
> For in it you can burn coal, wood or patent fuel,
> Put in your meat and then you'll find it will soon be doing;
> And when lighted away it goes and everything in motion;
> For Soyer's patent, I confess, it is a perfect creation.
> > Steam! Steam!
>
> They gather round for to see the wonderful man who made it,
> And stand in amaze and have a gaze and then begin to inspect it.
> All the cocked hats, I believe, say it's a stunning notion;
> For Soyer's patent, I confess, it is a perfect creation.
> > Steam! Steam!
>
> It's greatly approved of, I believe, by all the nation,
> And they are about to contract for this great invention.
> I sincerely hope there's no harm in anything I mention,
> For Soyer's patent, I confess, it is a perfect creation.
> > Steam! Steam!

This effusion was applauded and encored, and when Soyer
was seen in the theatre the whole audience rose and cheered,
demanding a speech. Much affected, he thanked them heartily,
and assured them that everyone from the queen downwards
hoped that they 'would live well and long, grow fat and die
happy'.

Lord Gough came out to distribute the Order of the Bath, and the stoves were exhibited for his benefit. Two soldiers, unassisted, cooked a very satisfactory dinner for the six hundred men of the 56th Regiment and the inspecting generals. The armies quickly diminished; the deserted huts were tenanted by hordes of rats, and every night robbers visited the remaining huts and tents to steal whatever they could lay hands on, getting bolder as the camp emptied.

Soyer felt it his duty to remain until the last of his stoves was packed and embarked, but he found the sudden change from overwork to idleness depressing, and made a trip (chronicled as usual in a letter to *The Times*) to Odessa. On his return he found that his people had been compelled by the increasing boldness of the bands of thieves to leave the 'Villarette' on Cathcart's Hill. He found it broken down, and Russell's adjacent hut was also ruined. A long, sad day was spent making a tour of the deserted camps; everything was burned, broken and despoiled.

At the last moment Soyer delayed to buy the rough carriage in which Miss Nightingale had travelled so many miles. By day and night she had gone from hospital to hospital in it, covering amazing distances, completely fearless and untiring. Soyer could not bear to let her carriage be auctioned with a motley collection of light carts and harness. He had it shipped to Southampton, where the mayor kept it until the *chef* himself returned to present it to Miss Nightingale. Fifty years later it was still preserved, with other Crimean relics, at her old home Lea Hurst.

A young Russian serf, an orphan, was found hidden on the ship that carried Soyer to Scutari. The boy declared that he had been ill-treated by his owner's agent, and since some English gentlemen had once given him money for holding their horses, he had determined to try to follow these kind people to their own country. Rather than turn the boy adrift in Constantinople, Soyer took charge of him, sent him to be bathed, invented a livery for him, and eventually brought him back to England as a devoted servant.

Soon the hospitals at Scutari were closed; Soyer's mission was at an end. To his delight he was granted a personal interview with the Sultan, to whom he presented a stove and a set of gorgeously bound copies of his works. A report appeared in the *Journal de Constantinople* that the Sultan had given him in return a magnificent snuff-box, but if it was ever sent, it did not reach Soyer. He collected a final bunch of testimonials from the doctors and the ambassador, and was once more free.

Securely packed in his luggage he now had an amazing collection of letters in praise of his Crimean labours and his stove. They range from General Windham's laconic 'After doubting many of your enthusiastic views as to cooking, I acknowledge that I am fairly beaten. Everyone to his trade', to Rokeby's polite acceptance of a Magic Stove—'I perceive it will henceforth be the means of my eating after a civilised fashion, so long as I have a coat pocket to carry it in'—the letter accompanying 'an inkstand made with a Russian grape-shot', sent as 'an assurance of the value I attach to all the exertions and arrangements you have made to ameliorate the position of our brave soldiers'. Generals, surgeons, colonels, purveyors, the new commissary-general and the chief of staff, all united to praise the stove, its inventor, and his work.

Fresh projects were already simmering in Soyer's mind, among them the completion of a book on the war (published in 1857 as *Soyer's Culinary Campaign*), and the compiling of another, to be called *The Culinary Wonders of all Nations*, which he did not live to carry out. He travelled home circuitously, first spending three weeks sight-seeing in Constantinople. A letter on Turkish cooking went to *The Times*, and his subsequent wanderings through Malta, Germany and Italy and the big provincial towns in France were also marked by communications to the press. At Malta he met many of his Crimean friends, and was fêted by every regiment, till in self-defence he had to move on.

When he came to Meaux, he was saddened by the sight of his birthplace. All his family were dead, and the town seemed strange and much smaller than it had seemed twenty-six years before. In Paris, the Emperor received Soyer, and was so struck by the new stove that he ordered one to be set up in the Tuileries as a model for the French army, and he further requested Soyer to visit and report upon the public kitchens, the *Fourneaux de l'Impératrice*.

At the beginning of May 1857 he returned to England, where Panmure, pleased by his protégé's success, presented him with a handsome bonus. Soyer summed up his work when a friend asked him how he had managed to feed the army when rations had been so short. 'Dere is my miracle, Mr Boyd', said the *chef*, 'for I did make good dishes out of nothing.'

He was more than ever a celebrity. In a collection entitled *Our Miscellany*, there appeared with other parodies 'Camp Cookery, by Alicksus Sawder.' The accuracy of the imitation showed how diligently the writer had studied his original; Soyer's exactitude—'When it has boiled for 8 minutes 25 seconds, throw 11/15ths of a teaspoonful of salt into the water'—his cheap soup—'Collect all the eggshells you can find; boil them for two hours on the scale of two quarts of water to half-a-dozen eggshells; drink hot, but not too much at a time'—his optimism and seeming miracles—'Green Peas in a Crimean Winter: Boil half a pint of white peas and put on green spectacles'—nothing was forgotten.

At a dinner held in Soyer's honour, it was proposed to sing *God Save the Queen*, but someone rose to his feet and sang amid cheers and shouts of laughter:

> God save our jolly chef,
> Long live our noble chef,
>   God save Soyer!
> Crimea victorious,
> Always uproarious,
> To join in our choreus,
>   God save Soyer!

Alexis Soyer

Oh Ude, Vatel, arise!
Try Soyer's pigeon pies,
  And fricandeaux!
Confound their mayonnaise,
On him we throw our praise,
And worship his entremets,
  God save Soyer!

His choicest wine in store
On us he's pleased to pour,
  Long will we drink!
May he into our paws
Hand crab and lobster claws,
Gaining our whole applause,
  God save Soyer!

CHAPTER XVI

'ARS LONGA, VITA BREVIS'

'Le charbon nous tue, mais qu'importe? Moins de jours et plus de gloire.'
CARÊME

IT was so exciting to be home again, there were so many reunions with old friends, so many introductions to new ones, so many old schemes to be revived and new plans to be begun, so many dinners with congratulatory speeches, so many theatres to be visited after absence with new pleasure, such an unending round of business, that Soyer's weakened constitution rebelled. The effects of his Crimean illness could not be thrown off, and during the scant fifteen months he had left he rarely felt entirely well.

He retired to Virginia Water to finish the *Culinary Campaign* in peace. It was dedicated to Panmure, in gratitude (wrote the author) for the 'unlimited confidence' reposed in him during his work in the East, and when it appeared at the end of the summer it was favourably reviewed (*The Times* gave it two columns) and had quite a success. The completely new angle from which the war was seen caught the public fancy, and confirmed the author's reputation for originality.

The frontispiece showed a Soyer sadly different from the hearty, assured figure who had greeted his readers on the title-page of the *Shilling Cookery* less than three years before. His clothes, though still exaggerated, were less fantastic; the waistcoat was bound instead of embroidered, a neat tie had replaced the flowing cravat, and there was no impudent velvet cap, *à la zoug-zoug*, over one ear. These were minor indications of the change; the real alteration was in the face, the expression; he might have been not three, but ten years

197

older, and it was clear that he had been engaged on more serious business than the jolly parties over which the earlier Soyer was so eminently fitted to preside.

Though the war was over, Soyer's work for the army was hardly begun. Wonders had been done for the army in the field, but Miss Nightingale was far from satisfied; she turned her attention to conditions at home. The men were, in Fortescue's words, 'infamously housed, abominably over-crowded, and senselessly fed'. Miss Nightingale, in her report to the Royal Commission on the Health of the British Army, put it even more strongly. 'Our soldiers', she said, 'enlist to death in the barracks.'

The disclosures of this commission led to the appointment in October 1857 of the Barracks and Hospitals Sub-Commission, composed of three of Miss Nightingale's intimates; she was its inspiration and its driving force. Much emphasis was laid on diet. The quartermaster-general had told the com-missioners, 'The men live upon boiled meat for twenty-one years.' Soldiers spent their allowance for vegetables in payment to outside bakehouses for roasting their meat, so weary did they become of what Miss Nightingale called the 'everlasting sameness of ration, the eternal boiled meat'. Speaking of the hospitals in the East, she declared that 'no attempt was made to compose a better or more varied diet; hardly any, till the arrival of Soyer, to improve the system of cooking'. Permission was obtained to improve, as a begin-ning, the London barracks, and Miss Nightingale, who had already recommended the use of Soyer's stoves, now co-opted their inventor to organise schools of regimental and hospital cookery, to plan kitchens, to draw up schemes for general diets, and to compose particular receipts.

With the assistance of his friend Warriner, Soyer produced the booklet *Instructions to Military Hospital Cooks, in the Preparation of Diets for Sick Soldiers*, which was approved by the commissioners and adopted by all military hospitals. The

Government Emigration Commissioners asked him to write a small book of receipts for the use of poor emigrants on board ship; Soyer not only wrote the book, but invented special tea and coffee pots for them, and a baking-dish 'specially adapted to sea-going conditions'. A copy of the book was given by the commissioners to each mess of eight adults—it is doubtful whether they were generous enough to supply baking-dishes as well.

General Lord Rokeby took the chair when Soyer lectured on military dietetics at the United Services Institute, and so famous had the *chef* become that it was the most crowded lecture of the session. To an applauding audience he outlined the conditions he had found, and those he had left, in the commissariat department; he described proposed reforms in naval cookery, on the lines of his scheme already approved by the Emigration Commissioners, and he talked of receipts he had arranged from the rations given to soldiers on service in India.

He was chosen as a member of the Government committee appointed to choose a cooking-wagon for an army on the march. Models and diagrams of every kind were examined; to each there was some insuperable objection. Soyer then produced a design of his own; the committee agreed unanimously that it was superior to all the others, and a specimen was built at Woolwich.

Remembering the horrors which had appeared at the front labelled 'Preserved Meat', and the earlier scandal of the meat supplied to the navy, Soyer invented a successful preserving and canning process of his own. He obtained a contract to supply part of the French army with this patent meat, and at the time of his death the English military authorities—always less hasty in the adoption of innovations—were thinking of using it in the English army.

Wellington Barracks, in Birdcage Walk, was chosen as the place for an experimental model kitchen, and there Soyer's original *batterie de cuisine*, which had seen such arduous service

Soyer at Wellington Barracks (from *The Illustrated London News*)

in the Crimea, was set up. On 28th July 1858, a crowd of military notabilities assembled; Soyer was given rations for three hundred men and invited to do his best.

From the 'three or four unpretending looking cylinders'—as the *Morning Chronicle* described them—he produced, instead of the usual invariable insipid soup and tasteless meat, a series of delicious dishes. Pea soup, salt pork with cabbage, stewed beef dumplings, roast mutton and beef, fried potatoes, sauté beef and mutton and liver, rice pudding and boiled rice, fried liver and bacon—it was as startling as a conjuring trick. Lord Rokeby straightway suggested that he should soon repeat the feat on a larger scale, and cook dinner for a whole battalion of the Guards. But the chosen battalion never got their dinner; within a week of his triumph Soyer was dead.

All this time, while attending endless committees, writing his various booklets on diet, inventing pots and pans and cooking-wagons, Soyer had been anything but well.

He never recovered completely from the shock of a nasty accident which happened in the summer of 1857. He had arranged to ride down to Virginia Water to picnic with a large party of friends, but when his horse was brought round it was fresh and restive. His secretary advised him to go by train, but this wounded Soyer's vanity—what! should an old campaigner who had ridden miles over the Crimean wastes on mules and ponies and chargers go ignominiously by train? Never. He indignantly mounted and rode off. The horse was soon completely out of control; it bolted in Kensington Road, and, alarmed by the shouts and wavings of passers-by, threw its rider, who was dragged along by one leg for some distance. Miraculously, no bones were broken, and he insisted on going on to his friends. They were beginning to wonder what had happened to him, when a hansom was seen coming furiously towards them, and in it, bruised, torn, dusty, shaken, but indomitable, was Soyer. For several weeks he was kept in bed, and he was lame for months, but as soon as he was able to hobble about he began again his incredibly busy round.

In the spring of 1858 he became seriously ill, and often spat blood. Against all advice and persuasion he continued to work and play as hard as ever. At the end of May he organised the refreshments at a grand bazaar in aid of the wives and children of soldiers and sailors, and met there many old Crimean friends (among them jolly Mother Seacole, stout and flourishing as ever), whose invitations were accepted and crowded into a programme already over-full.

When forced, because he was too weak to stand upright, to stay in bed, he would agree to take advice, and promise to be patient, to go abroad, to rest, to be quiet, to diet himself as well as the rest of the world. But as soon as he was well enough to travel, there was always just one vital reason why he must stay just one more day in England. 'You know, my dear fellow, how urgent it is that I should finish my hospital dietary'—'If I stay until my barracks kitchen is opened, then when I return, rested, a new man, I will find my system in full working order.' As if he knew how short his life was to be, he filled every minute with business, and so doing shortened it still further.

Invention in one's own sphere was so easy, surely some doctor had found a panacea, surely some chemist had compounded an elixir which could cure him, so he consulted all sorts of medicine men, from his orthodox Crimean doctors to the most blatant of quacks. Two or three doctors would visit him in a day, and even when weakest he would take a keen delight in planning their visits so that they would not meet, and in seeing Doctor A's nostrums whisked into a cupboard before they could offend the eye of Doctor B.

June came, but under this crazy regimen he still grew thinner and weaker, and yet still did not lose hope. On 19th June, however, he made a simple will, leaving some of Emma's pictures to the National Gallery, and to his friends Mr Crosse and Mr Blackwell. Fifty pounds went to an infant niece, and a hundred were to be invested, and the income used for the upkeep of Emma's tomb. Everything else he left to his faithful housekeeper, Sophia Cooke, who had been with him for many years.

Whenever he was well enough to rise, he would pop into his kitchen. The familiar and beloved scene was an immediate tonic; he would merrily cry that all was going to rack and ruin without him, stir a pot, taste a sauce, call for his apron and concoct a savoury mess in a saucepan, and eat and drink what was forbidden. He might even venture out to a smoking concert at the 'Albion'—conveniently opposite the stage door of Drury Lane—or join the select circle in the snug little back parlour at Frost's, where his friends sat packed as tight as sardines to hear his tales of the war and the peace and the world, to laugh at his jokes and applaud his songs.

Inevitably collapse followed; in the morning the doctors had to be sent for and the whole mad business began over again. It was in direct defiance of his doctors' orders that he opened his model kitchen at Wellington Barracks on 28th July, but his great success, with its accompaniment of private and press compliments, seemed to give him new life.

The Crystal Palace Company had borrowed some of Madame Soyer's pictures for an exhibition, and he wanted to go and see that they had been well hung. The Paxton Hotel at Norwood was run by one of his friends, and there he was to stay. On Monday, 2nd August, he amused himself at the exhibition; as ever, he did not know when to stop, and came back completely tired out. The next morning he felt well enough to plan a dinner-party for Wednesday night, even commissioning a friend to bring down a special dessert from town.

But on Tuesday evening he became very weak and drowsy, and though he swore that this was merely the result of a careless dose of a prescribed sleeping draught, his friends became thoroughly alarmed. With great difficulty he was got back to his own house in St John's Wood. He suffered much during the night, but in the morning fell into a coma, and lay unconscious until the evening of 5th August. Three of his old friends watched beside him as he lay, unfamiliar, silent, still; late in the evening he opened his eyes, and they hoped to hear him speak; but without coming to, he died.

EPILOGUE

'Toute sa vie fut consacrée aux arts utiles.'

Epitaph of Véry the restaurateur

'HIS DEATH', wrote Miss Nightingale, 'is a great disaster. Others have studied cooking for the purposes of gormandising, some for show, but none but he for the purpose of cooking large quantities of food in the most nutritious manner for great numbers of men. He has no successor.' To her, characteristically, the work came first, and she mourned its cessation. Soyer's hosts of friends mourned more the man, the gay companion, the quick-witted jester, the kind master and loyal friend.

He was buried as he had wished, beside Emma, close to the monument of which he had been so proud; though little notice was given of his funeral, and its time was changed at the last moment, a great crowd of colleagues and friends assembled. The service ended, and everyone turned away. Suddenly Charles Pierce, Soyer's oldest friend, who had been with him when he died, stepped forward and said with great emotion:

'Oh my dear friend, my long loved friend Soyer! we may not part from thee thus without giving utterance to our deep regrets at leaving thee, and pouring forth our blessings on thy memory. Oh friend! Oh companion, often tried and never found wanting—great in heart—fresh in spirit—bright in genius and simple-minded, who can tell thy worth? who can hope to repair thy loss?

'Farewell, dear friend! Farewell! Adieu, Alexis, thou kindest and dearest of men! thou noblest of Frenchmen!'

So spoke this old friend at the moment of loss. Another dear friend, George Augustus Sala, shall have the last word about '... the kindly, erratic, frivolous, warm-hearted Alexis Soyer.... He was a vain man; but he was good, and kind, and charitable.... Alexis always had his pensioners and his alms-duns, to whom his hand was ever open. He was but a Cook; but he was my dear and good friend. He quacked, certainly—puffed himself and his eccentricity in all kinds of ways—in dress, manners, speech, mode of life; but he never derogated one iota from his dignity as an honest man.

'He was no vulgar charlatan, for he was full of inventive ingenuity; and to the soldier's and poor man's kitchen his maxims, if properly carried out, would be even now in-estimably beneficial. He was an original. He didn't do anybody any harm. He did, on the contrary, a vast amount of good in his generation; and even those who laughed at him, loved him for his simple childlike ways and generous candour. Princes used to shake hands with Alexis; but he never bragged of his grand acquaintances, or deceived himself for one moment with the notion that he was looked upon as aught else than a good-humoured dependent. He never curried favour, never toadied, was never impertinent; but knew his own place, exacted the meed of respect due to him, and when the grandees came to see him in his kitchen, let them know that not alone *savetier*, but *cuisinier*, was *maître chez soi*. Peace be to his ashes; for he was the worthiest of souls.'

THE END

APPENDICES

APPENDIX A

DIALOGUE CULINAIRE

Entre Lord M. H. *et* A. Soyer

S. Vous avez parfaitement raison, Mylord; le titre de gourmet n'appartient qu'à celui qui mange avec art, avec science, avec ordre, et même avec beaucoup d'ordre.

Lord M. Le gourmand n'est jamais gourmet; l'un mange sans déguster, l'autre déguste en mangeant.

S. L'homme fier et hautain, Mylord, s'occupe de son dîner par besoin; l'homme de monde, épicure profond, s'en occupe avec plaisir.

Lord M. Il est certain que l'on ne saurait donner trop d'attention à la rigide exécution et à l'ordre intelligent d'un dîner. Le dîner étant de chaque jour, de chaque saison, de chaque siècle, est non seulement la seule mode héréditaire, mais aussi l'âme de la sociabilité; lisez l'histoire, et vous y verrez que de tous les temps, et chez tous les peuples, le bien qui s'est fait, et quelquefois le mal, fut toujours précédé ou suivi d'un copieux dîner.

S. Rien n'est plus vrai, Mylord, que de tous les plaisirs de la vie qui nous sont légués en ce monde, celui de la table est le seul auquel les rênes du char de la vie n'échappent qu'à regret; et souvent, un ami fidèle ne les lâche qu'aux abords du tombeau; tandis que tous les autres s'épanouissent frivolement, comme à la suite d'un beau printemps, et, en nous délaissant, couvrent nos fronts radieux du givre des ans.

Lord M. Il est positif que déguster est une faculté de tout âge; un vieillard de cent six ans, que j'ai beaucoup connu, dégustait parfaitement alors.

S. Nos cent dégustateurs demandent de continuelles études, et réclament, sans cesse, un continuel changement.

Lord M. Le plus bel esprit manquerait d'éloquence s'il négligeait par trop l'ordre de ses repas.

S. C'est ce qui nous prouve, Mylord, que nos plus agréables sensations dépendent non seulement de la nature, mais aussi du soin que nous donnons à notre personne.

Lord M. Oui, car plus l'âme est sensible, plus la dégustation est féconde. Les sensations dégustatives opèrent avec autant d'activité sur le palais que le charme de la mélodie le fait sur l'ouïe; par exemple, l'homme dans un cas de folie, peut bien éprouver le besoin de manger, mais l'action enchanteresse de la dégustation lui est aussi interdite que la raison.

S. Votre argument sur ce point est extrêmement juste, Mylord. N'êtes-vous pas aussi de mon avis, que rien ne dispose mieux l'esprit humain à des transactions amicales, qu'un dîner bien conçu et artistement préparé.

Lord M. C'est ce qui m'a toujours fait dire qu'un bon cuisinier est aussi utile qu'un savant conseiller.

S. Je me suis toujours aperçu, Mylord, que le palais le plus fin était le plus difficile à plaire, mais aussi le plus juste à récompenser.

Lord M. Le choix des vins est de haute importance dans l'ordre d'un dîner; un vin fin, léger et généreux protège le cuisinier et devient le bienfaiteur du convive.

S. Permettez-moi de vous faire observer, Mylord, qu'une réunion gastronomique sans dames est à mes yeux un parterre sans fleurs, l'océan sans flots, une flotte maritime sans voiles.

Lord M. Certes, de telles réunions sont le berceau des bonnes mœurs et de la jovialité, comme la débauche est le tombeau de la moralité.

Reform Club
14*th* May 1846

APPENDIX B

MENU OF BANQUET
GIVEN AT THE REFORM CLUB TO
IBRAHIM PASHA
3rd July 1846

SEIZE POTAGES

Quatre à la Victoria
Quatre à la Comte de Paris
Quatre à la Louis Philippe
Quatre à la Colbert, aux Légumes Printaniers

SEIZE POISSONS

Quatre de Turbots, sauce à la Mazarin
Quatre de Saumons de Severn à la Crème
Quatre de Buissons de Filets de Merlans à l'Égyptienne
Quatre de Truites Saumonées en Matelote Marinère

SEIZE RELEVÉS

Quatre de Chapons à la Nelson
Quatre de Saddleback de Southdown Mouton, rôti à la Soyer
Quatre de Poulardes en Diadême
Quatre de Saddleback d'Agneau, rôti à la Sévigné

Baron of Beef à l'Anglais
Entrée pagodatique de riz à la Luxor

CINQUANTE-QUATRE ENTRÉES

Six de Poussins Printaniers à l'Ambassadrice
Six de Côtelettes de Mouton à la Reform
Quatre de Riz de Veau piquées en Macédoine de Légumes
Quatre de Petits Vol-au-Vents aux Laitances de Maquereaux
Quatre de Timballes de Riz au Queues d'Agneau
Quatre de Jambonneaux Braisés au Vin de Madère

Quatre de Volailles Farcies à la Russe aux Légumes Verts
Quatre de Pâtés Chauds de Cailles à la Banquière
Quatre de Rissolettes à la Pompadour
Quatre de Grenadins de Bœuf à la Beyrout
Quatre de Turbans Épigramme de Levreau au Fumet
Six de Côtelettes d'Agneau à la Vicomtesse

SEIZE RÔTS

Quatre de Turkey Poult Piqués et Bardés
Quatre de Gros Chapons au Cresson
Quatre de Canetons au Jus de Bigardes
Quatre de Levreaux au Jus de Groseilles

CINQUANTE-QUATRE ENTREMENTS

Six de Gelées Macédoine de Fruits au Dantzic
Six de Croquantes d'Amandes aux Cerises
Six de Tartelettes Pralines aux Abricots
Quatre Turbans de Meringues Demi-Glacées
Quatre de Charlotte Prussienne
Quatre de Galatines à la Volière
Quatre de Mirotons de Homard à l'Indienne
Quatre de Salades de Volaille à la Soyer
Quatre de Haricots Verts au Beurre Noisette
Quatre de Pain de Pêches au Noyeau
Quatre de Petits Pois à l'Anglo-Français
Quatre de Gelées Cristallisées à l'Ananas

RELEVÉS DE RÔTS

CRÈME D'ÉGYPTE À L'IBRAHIM PASHA
GÂTEAU BRITANNIQUE À L'AMIRAL
Quatre de Jabous Glacés en Surprise
Deux de Meringues Chinoises-Pagoda aux Fraises
Quatre de Côtelettes en Surprise à la Reform
Quatre de Manivaux de Champignons au Curaçao en Surprise

APPENDIX C

DINER LUCULLUSIAN A LA SAMPAYO

REFORM CLUB.

9 Mai, 1846.   *Diner pour* 10 *Personnes.*

Potage à la Comte de Paris.
Do. à la purée d'Asperges.

Deux Poissons.

Saumon de Severne   Rougets gratinés
à la Mazarin.   à la Montesquieu.

Deux Relevés.

Le Chapon farci de Foie gras à la Nelson.
Saddleback d'Agneau de Maison à la Sévigné.

Quatre Hors-d'œuvres à la Française.

Les Olives farcies.   Salade d'Anchois historiée.
Thon mariné à l'Italienne.   Sardines à l'Huile de Noisette.

Quatre Entrées.

Sauté de Filets de Volaille à l'Ambassadrice.
Petites Croustades de Beurre aux Laitances de Maquereaux.
Cotelettes de Mouton Galloise à la Réforme.
Turban de Ris de Veau purée de Concombres.

Rissolettes à la Pompadour. *(left margin)*   *Rissolettes à la Pompadour.* *(right margin)*

Deux Rôts.

Les Dotrelles aux Feuilles de Vignes.
Le Buisson d'Ecrevisse Pagodatique, au Vin
de Champagne à la Sampayo.

La Gelée de Dantzic   Les Croquantes d'Amandes
aux fruits Printaniers.   pralinées aux Abricots.
Les petits Pois nouveaux   Le Miroton de Homard aux
à l'Anglo-Français.   Œufs de Pluviers.
Les grosses Truffes   La Crème mousseuse au
à l'essence de Madère.   Curaçao.

Les grosses Asperges vertes, sauce à la Crème. *(left margin)*   *Les grosses Asperges vertes, sauce à la Crème.* *(right margin)*

Deux Relevés.

La Hûre de Sanglier demi-glacée,
garnie de Champignons en surprise.
Les Diablotins au fromage de Windsor.

APPENDIX D

PROSPECTUS FOR SOYER'S UNIVERSAL SYMPOSIUM

GORE HOUSE KENSINGTON

Season Tickets

Single Ticket .... .One Guinea
Double Ticket .... One and a Half Guineas
Family Ticket admitting Five .... Three Guineas

None of which are Transferable

To be had at MR MITCHELL's Royal Library, *Bond Street*, SAMS's LIBRARY, *St James's Street*, and all the principal LIBRARIES and MUSIC SELLERS.

The tickets will admit to all parts of this monstre and unique establishment, which is capable of providing dinners and refreshments of every description for five or six thousand persons daily, the charges for which will not preclude persons of every station from partaking of the hospitality of the Maison Soyer.

Among the numerous attractions of this extraordinary Mansion and Grounds (which enclose the famous and park-like Pré D'Orsay) are:

Le Vestibule de la Fille de l'Orage—The Hall of Architectural Wonders—The Blessington Temple of the Muses—The Temple of Danae, or the Shower of Gems—The Transatlantic Passage—Le Forêt Péruvienne, or the Night of Stars—The Grand Staircase, containing the Macédoine of all Nations, being a Demisemitragicomigrotesquepanofanifunnisymposiorama, or Such-a-getting-upstairs-to-the-Great-Exhibition-of-1851, Painted in Fresco by MR GEORGE AUGUSTUS SALA—The Gallic Pavilion, or l'Avenue des Amours—The Temple of Phoebus—The Glittering Rocaille of Eternal Snow—The Bower of Ariadne—The Door of the Dungeon of Mystery—The Boudoir de la Vallière, or the Doriana—L'Œil de Bœuf, or Flora's Retreat—The Celestial Hall of Golden Lilies—The Grand Banqueting Bridge, al Fresco—The Washington Refreshment Room, for the dispensing of every sort of American Beverage—Soyer's Colossal Offering to Amphitrite—

Cupid's Delight—The Impenetrable Grotto of Ondine—Hebe's Mistake, or the Enchanted Fountain—The Aerial Orchestra—The Baronial Hall, containing the late MADAME SOYER's celebrated Pictures, and the complete Gallery of eminent Characters by COUNT D'ORSAY, munificently presented to M. SOYER by J. MITCHELL ESQ., of Bond Street—Gigantic Encampment of All Nations, with Monster Tablecloth, 307 feet long, of British manufacture—Picnic Tents—Magic Cookery, by Soyer's Original Lilliputian Kitchen—Marble Statues and Fountains—Bacchanalian Vases—Emerald Pyramids of Morning Dew—Gipsy Dell—and Statuettes à la Watteau, etc.

Subscribers will be permitted to view, from 12 till 2 o'clock, the Symposium Kitchen, in which no less than 600 Joints can be cooked with ease in the course of the day.

APPENDIX E

CHRISTMAS DINNER IN HAM YARD TO 22,000 OF THE POOR

9000 pounds of roast and baked meat

178   beef pies
50   hare pies
60   rabbit pies
50   pork and mutton pies

Each weighed between ten and thirty pounds; one of them, the 'monster pie', weighed sixty pounds

20   roast geese
5000   pints of porter
3300   pounds of potatoes
5000   pounds of plum pudding
50   cakes
6000   half-quartern loaves
1   cask of biscuits
18   bushels of Spanish nuts
18   bushels of chestnuts
6   boxes of oranges
3000   two-ounce packages of tea
3000   three-ounce packages of coffee
5000   half-pounds of sugar

and

One whole ox, roasted by gas—the gas supplied by the Western Gas Company, under the gratuitous superintendence of MR INSPECTOR DAVIES of that establishment.

INDEX

Relevant entries are grouped under the following headings: Banquets, *Chefs* and Cooks, Clubs, Eating-houses Restaurants and Taverns, Periodicals cited, Soup-kitchens, Works by Soyer.

Index

Index

Index

Index

THE GAMEKEEPER AT HOME and
THE AMATEUR POACHER

RICHARD JEFFERIES

With an introduction by Richard Fitter

First published in 1878 and 1879, these two books nostalgically recapture the sights, characters, and pastimes of the nineteenth-century English countryside.

THE DIARY OF A COUNTRY PARSON

JAMES WOODFORDE

Edited by John Beresford

James Woodforde was an eighteenth-century Norfolk parson, a *bon vivant* with a passion for food and a healthy appetite for drink, sport, and gossip. Ever since its discovery early this century, his classic diary has entranced readers with its vivid portrait of daily life in the rural England of two centuries ago.

A LONDON FAMILY BETWEEN THE WARS

M. V. HUGHES

The Hughes family – a widow with three sons – were not well off financially, but were rich in affection. This is a gentle, often humorous account of a family growing up in the rural environs of London in the 1920s and 1930s. It recaptures the charms of a now vanished world, in which *The Times* arrives by bicycle, household necessities are supplied by a hawker with a pony cart, and making a telephone call is an adventure.

THE AUTOBIOGRAPHY OF A SUPER-TRAMP

W. H. DAVIES

With a preface by George Bernard Shaw

This is the classic account of the poet W. H. Davies's adventures as a young man travelling around America and England at the turn of the century. His spare, evocative prose gives raw power to his experiences among tricksters, down-and-outs, and itinerant labourers, and makes the characters he encounters – New Haven Baldy, the Indian Kid, and Boozy Bob – unforgettable.

THE DIARY OF A GEORGIAN SHOPKEEPER

Thomas Turner

With an introduction by G. H. Jennings

'I cannot say I came home sober.' Recurrent drunkenness (and attendant guilt) might be called the leading theme of the diary of Thomas Turner of East Hoathly in Sussex, a most candid, perceptive, entertaining personal document with unique social and historical overtones. The subjects Turner touches on are many and very various: his activities as shopkeeper, churchwarden, and Overseer to the Parish Vestry; the principal historical events of the period (1754–65), with Turner's (often unexpected) reactions to them; reflections on marriage; accounts of his first wife's illness and death, and of his courting of a new wife; the races, cockfighting, cricket; poverty, boredom, illness, and death; and of course continual drinking.

MAD SHEPHERDS

L. P. Jacks

Snarley Bob is the main character in this series of stories set in the Cotswold village of Deadborough at the turn of the century. Gruff and often rude to people he considers foolish, at other times gentle, and always wise, he can understand the song of the nightingale and the movements of the stars. This empathy with nature is his philosophy of life, known to others as 'snarleychology'. Among the other figures who appear are Shoemaker Hankin, an ardent atheist who has read the works of J. S. Mill, and the parson's wife Mrs Abel, who used to be an actress and is considered 'not proper' by her well-to-do neighbours. The author, one-time Dean of Manchester College, Oxford, has a dry sense of humour which makes *Mad Shepherds* charming and unsentimental; it was first published in 1910.

SMALL TALK AT WREYLAND

Cecil Torr

With an introduction by Jack Simmons

In 1916 Cecil Torr began to record the character and history of Wreyland, a tiny hamlet on the edge of Dartmoor where he lived. By drawing on the letters and diaries of his father and grandfather, as well as on his own eccentric memory, he provided a chronicle of about 150 years. His aim was to preserve the wealth of local knowledge still retained by the older natives, but he wanders from idea to idea in *Small Talk*, butting in on his own narrative with such words as 'I once spent a night on the summit of Etna . . .'. *Small Talk* is full of fascinatingly incongruous anecdotes, but it is most importantly an exact diary of Devonshire life, correct to the minutest detail. A contemporary reviewer commented in the *New Statesman*: 'I do not know any book in which so many characteristic and uniformly good stories of Devonshire folk are to be found.'

A VICTORIAN POACHER

James Hawker's Journal

Life was hard in the mid-eighteenth century, especially for the son of a village tailor, so James Hawker took to poaching. To the day of his death at the age of 84 he continued to outwit the exasperated, yet admiring gamekeepers of the Leicestershire estates he plundered. His diary reveals him to be a shrewd, vigorous, and humorous man, and speaks eloquently of country lore, wildlife, and the poacher's craft.

STILL GLIDES THE STREAM

Flora Thompson

Like her well-loved trilogy *Lark Rise to Candleford*, this book depicts the vanished life of the countryside which Flora Thompson knew as a child in the 1880s. Cast in a fictional form, it is an enchanting portrait of an Oxfordshire village and its inhabitants around the time of Queen Victoria's Golden Jubilee.

'reading it is a perfect pleasure'   Benny Green

THE WESTERN ISLAND or
THE GREAT BLASKET

Robin Flower

Covering the years 1910 to 1930, this is an illustrated account of the folklore and life of the Great Blasket Island, three miles out into the Atlantic to the west of County Kerry.

AN OLD WOMAN'S REFLECTIONS

PEIG SAYERS

'The Queen of Gaelic story-tellers' spent the greater part of her long life on the Great Blasket Island. Here she reflects on the days of her youth spent on her beloved island.

THE ISLANDMAN

TOMÁS Ó CROHAN

Tomás Ó Crohan was born on the Great Blasket Island in 1856 and died there in 1937, a great master of his native Irish. His account of the harsh life there is a valuable and fascinating record of a now vanished way of life.